PROPHETIC
GUIDE
to the
END TIMES

PROPHETIC GUIDE
to the
END TIMES

Facing the Future without Fear

DEREK PRINCE

Chosen
Grand Rapids, Michigan

Published by Chosen Books
A division of Baker Publishing Group
P.O. Box 6287, Grand Rapids, MI 49516-6287
www.chosenbooks.com

Second printing, June 2008

Printed in the United States of America

Library of Congress Cataloging-in-Publication Data
Prince, Derek.
    Prophetic guide to the end times : facing the future without fear / Derek
Prince.
        p.   cm.
    Includes index.
    ISBN 978-0-8007-9445-3 (pbk.)
    1. Bible—Prophecies—End of the world. 2. End of the world—Biblical
teaching. 3. Bible—Prophecies—Second Advent. 4. Second Advent—Biblical teaching. I. Title.
BS649.E63P75 2008
236′.9—dc22   2007030192

Contents

1

The Bible Unveils
the Future

History tells us something unique about the human race: We have a great hunger to know what the future holds. Traditionally we have sought this knowledge by spiritual means that bypass our reason or capability, means such as astrology, pronouncements from oracles, fortune-telling and various forms of mysticism. These attempts have proved elusive and deceptive.

In recent times we have turned to more sophisticated and scientific ways to feed our craving. Experts in various fields—physics, sociology, economics, even population demographics and food production and weather prognostication—have conducted countless studies to shed light on the days to come. The results of these works, though thought-provoking and helpful, nevertheless simply verify the fact that no human mind or system can foresee the many contingencies that affect future events. For this reason, none of these studies can be accepted as fully reliable.

There remains, however, a third source to which we may look for revelation about the future. This third source is faultless in its reliability. It is the Bible, and within its pages lie the prophetic insights we seek. Only the Word of God can satisfy our longing to see into the future.

First and foremost, we must understand that the Bible offers light to those who study it and obey it. A number of Scriptures make this point, including the familiar words of the psalmist to the Lord: "Your word is a lamp to my feet and a light to my path" (Psalm 119:105). In order to have forward mobility, we generally require feet to walk with and a path to walk on. But in order to move forward with confidence, it helps to see where we are going. God's Word provides light for our feet and light for our path. In other words, the Bible shows us where to step next. It may not always show us a long way ahead, but we are never left to walk in darkness. What a tremendous blessing that is! If we study and obey the Bible, we will never be left walking in darkness.

With this universal desire to know what the future holds, we might think that believers, who consider the Bible God's inspired revelation of His will, would search its pages eagerly for understanding about the period immediately preceding the return of the Lord—the time referred to as "the last days" in at least half the books of the Bible. In my contact with Christians of different nationalities, denominations and backgrounds, however, I have found just the opposite to be true. I have consistently run into an altogether inadequate appreciation of the importance of biblical prophecy! I recognize that some Christians have been turned off by so-called prophets who have made predictions in the name of the Lord, including the exact date Jesus is due to return. Because this happens from time to time in the history of the Church, people get turned off and say, "If that's what prophecy is like, I don't want any part of it."

That is a disastrous conclusion because Christians need to understand biblical prophecy. Why can I say this with assurance? Because at least one-quarter of the Bible is predictive prophecy. We cannot afford to ignore one-quarter of the Bible and expect to receive all that God has for us. Let's look at what God Himself says in regard to His prophetic word.

God Reveals the Future

Throughout the Bible, God actually claims to foretell the future within its pages. Look at these passages from the book of Isaiah.

> "This is what the LORD says—Israel's King and Redeemer, the LORD Almighty: I am the first and I am the last; apart from me there is no God. Who then is like me? Let him proclaim it. Let him declare and lay out before me what has happened since I established my ancient people, and what is yet to come—yes, let him foretell what will come."
>
> Isaiah 44:6–7, NIV

The Lord presents a challenge here: "I am God. I know what happened in the past; I know what will happen in the future. If anybody repudiates this, let him come forth with the same breadth of factual information that I offer." Then in the next verse, God says to His people: "Do not tremble, do not be afraid. Did I not proclaim this and foretell it long ago?" (verse 8, NIV).

Those who do make claims of predictions through "alternative" sources of information are easily shown to be impostors. To the astrologers, fortune-tellers and soothsayers—of whom there were multitudes in biblical days, just as there are today—the Lord says this:

> "This is what the LORD says—your Redeemer, who formed you in the womb: I am the LORD, who has made all things, who alone stretched out the heavens, who spread out the earth by myself, who foils the signs of false prophets and makes fools of diviners [fortune-tellers], who overthrows the learning of the wise and turns it into nonsense, who carries out the words of his servants and fulfills the predictions of his messengers."
>
> Isaiah 44:24–26, NIV

When God's servants predict, God stands behind what they say and sees that it happens. But when false prophets predict, God turns their words upside down and makes them look foolish. Only God's Word will stand—His purpose alone is the one that will be worked out. Almighty God is speaking in these verses, the One who created the heavens, created the earth, created mankind and all things. He is in full control of all that He brought into being.

> "Remember the former things, those of long ago; I am God, and there is no other; I am God, and there is none like me. I make known the end from the beginning, from ancient times,

what is still to come. I say: My purpose will stand, and I will do all that I please."

Isaiah 46:9–10, NIV

If we believe God alone can reveal the future, it follows that we must gain a right appreciation of His sovereignty, majesty and justice. God never makes mistakes. Everything He does is right. We may have gone through situations that left us wondering if He was being unfair, but that is impossible. God is always just and always right.

Here is a passage of Scripture I like to speak as a proclamation. It is taken from two chapters of Daniel and declares the sovereign majesty of God.

"Blessed be the name of God forever and ever, for wisdom and might are His. And He changes the times and the seasons; He removes kings and raises up kings; He gives wisdom to the wise and knowledge to those who have understanding. He reveals deep and secret things; He knows what is in the darkness, and light dwells with Him."

. . . For His dominion is an everlasting dominion, and His kingdom is from generation to generation. All the inhabitants of the earth are reputed as nothing; He does according to His will in the army of heaven and among the inhabitants of the earth. No one can restrain His hand or say to Him, "What have You done?"

Daniel 2:20–22; 4:34–35

The last two verses are the words of Nebuchadnezzar, who went through a pretty difficult time to come to that realization. He spent seven years like an animal out in the wild. His hair grew like a bird's feathers, his nails like an animal's

11

claws, and he fed on grass. But at the end of seven years God restored everything that Nebuchadnezzar had lost.

By then Nebuchadnezzar had become a different man, transformed by the school of God's discipline. This was his testimony: "Your dominion is an everlasting dominion. All the inhabitants of the earth are reputed as nothing. You do according to Your will in the army of heaven and among the inhabitants of the earth. No one can restrain Your hand." Though he had ruled as the most powerful monarch on earth at that time, Nebuchadnezzar came to realize there was One infinitely more powerful than he. That One was the God of Israel. This knowledge of God's sovereignty is an essential basis for approaching biblical prophecy.

Proof That His Prophecies Are True

If we have any further doubts about God's ability or plans to reveal the future to us through the Bible, we need only look at His record. Given below are two prominent examples: predictions made concerning the life of Jesus and the nation of Israel. These are just a handful of the many predictions made thousands of years ago that have been and are still being accurately fulfilled in every detail.

The Life of Jesus Christ

Words spoken through God's prophets, as recorded in the Old Testament, foretold every significant event in the life of Jesus in accurate detail. When each one of these prophecies came true, the Bible says that it happened "that the Scripture might be fulfilled." Here are eighteen specific events in the life of Jesus as predicted in the Old Testament and shown to be fulfilled in the Gospel accounts of Jesus' life.

His birth of a virgin (Isaiah 7:14; Matthew 1:24–25).

His birth at Bethlehem (Micah 5:2; Luke 2:4–7).

His flight into Egypt (Hosea 11:1; Matthew 2:15).

His being anointed by the Holy Spirit (Isaiah 61:1; Matthew 3:16).

His ministry in Galilee (Isaiah 9:1–2; Matthew 4:15–16).

His healing of the sick (Isaiah 61:1; John 5:1–9).

His use of parables (Psalm 78:2; Matthew 13:34–35).

His being betrayed by a friend (Psalm 41:9; John 13:18).

His being forsaken by His disciples (Psalm 88:8; Mark 14:50).

His being hated without a cause (Psalm 35:19; John 15:25).

His being rejected by the Jews (Isaiah 53:3; John 1:11).

His being condemned with criminals (Isaiah 53:12; Luke 22:37).

His garments being parted and divided by lot (Psalm 22:18; Matthew 27:35).

His being offered vinegar for His thirst (Psalm 69:21; Matthew 27:48).

His body being pierced without His bones being broken (Psalm 34:20; John 19:36; also Zechariah 12:10; John 19:37).

His being buried in a rich man's tomb (Isaiah 53:9; Matthew 27:57–60).

His rising from the dead on the third day (Hosea 6:2;
Luke 24:46).

Scripture is unerring in all these points concerning the
life of Jesus.

The History of the Nation of Israel

Our second example of biblical prophecy involves the
history of the nation of Israel. Again, the examples are
far too numerous to list here, but suffice it to say that the
Bible has predicted the course of Israel's history accurately
for the past 3,500 years. Here are a few specific aspects
of Israel's history predicted in the Bible long before they
occurred:

Enslavement in Egypt (Genesis 15:13).

Deliverance with wealth from Egypt (Genesis 15:14).

Possession of the land of Canaan (Genesis 15:18–20).

Turning to idolatry there (Deuteronomy 32:15–21).

Center of worship in Jerusalem (Deuteronomy 12:5–6;
Psalm 132:13–14).

Assyrian captivity (Amos 5:27; 6:14; 7:17).

Babylonian captivity (Jeremiah 16:13; 21:10).

Destruction of the first Temple (2 Chronicles 7:19–22).

Return from Babylon (Isaiah 6:11–13; 48:20).

Destruction of the second Temple (Matthew 24:2; Luke
19:43–44).

Scattered among all nations (Leviticus 26:33–34; Ezekiel
12:15).

Persecution and oppression (Leviticus 26:36–39).

Regathering from all nations (Isaiah 11:11–12; Zechariah 10:9–10).

Here are a few predictions yet unfulfilled:

All nations against Jerusalem (Zechariah 12:2–3; 14:1–2).
Supernatural revelation of Messiah (Zechariah 12:10–14).
Messiah comes in glory (Zechariah 14:3–5).

In light of the Bible's proven record, we can turn to it confidently as our source for information about events still in the future. Remember, if we study and obey the Bible, we do not need to walk in darkness.

Giving Heed to Biblical Prophecy

This leaves us with one final question as we begin our study of end time prophecy in the Bible. What is the ultimate purpose? Why would God give us a book that tells us what is going to happen in the future? All of the prophecies throughout Scripture that have yet to occur have one central mission: to make us aware of the coming of the Lord as an imminent reality.

Let's look at just one verse from the second epistle of Peter. Peter has been writing about the revelation he and two other apostles had of Jesus on the Mount of Transfiguration when they saw the honor and glory God the Father had bestowed upon Jesus. Then he relates that there is something even more important: "We [also] have the prophetic word confirmed [made more sure], which you do well to heed as a light that shines in a dark place, until the day dawns and the morning star rises in your hearts" (2 Peter 1:19).

Peter is saying, in effect, "That revelation we had on the Mount of Transfiguration was wonderful. It was valid, and it is recorded now in Scripture. But there is something much more certain: It is the prophetic word of Scripture, the written prophecies of the Bible."

Let's make a crucial distinction. The gift of prophecy, which I esteem, believe in and from time to time exercise, comes from human agents and must be judged by Scripture. When we talk (as Peter does here) about the prophetic word given in Scripture, however, it is *not* to be judged. There is a great difference. Every word of God is pure, like silver purified in a furnace seven times (see Psalm 12:6). The written, prophetic word of God is totally and absolutely authoritative, and Peter says we do well to give heed to it. In other words, it is in our best interests to pay attention to it. If we fail to do so, we are depriving ourselves of an important provision of God for our lives.

We need to give heed to the prophetic word "until the day dawns and the morning star rises in [our] hearts." Peter is not talking about what is happening in the world; he is talking about what is happening in our hearts. Even if a person is a believer—saved, baptized in the Spirit and destined for heaven—that one will be walking in darkness here on earth if he ignores the light God has provided. Walking in darkness does not mean we will be refused entry into heaven when we die. But it does mean we will be stumbling and groping while here on earth, not understanding what is going on, fearful and confused.

During my service in World War II, I spent three years stationed in the deserts of North Africa. Most of that time we lived by the sun because we had no artificial sources of light. When it got dark, we went to bed. When it became light, we got up. During that time I observed some unique sights. One was that at certain seasons of the year when the sun was due to rise, the horizon would become luminous, growing quite light in that part of the heavens. You would think the sun was rising, but it was not the sun. It was the morning star called Aurora. It was an infallible sign: When Aurora rose, we knew that the sun was going to rise next. Peter says to let this Aurora—this morning star—rise in our hearts, because when it arises we will know for sure Jesus is coming back. God desires that every one of us live in excited anticipation of the return of the Lord. That is how every believer should be living.

As Hebrews 9:28 tells us, Jesus is going to appear for those who wait for Him eagerly. Are we waiting for Him eagerly? If the morning star has risen in our hearts, then we will be waiting for Him with great anticipation, and He will appear to us the second time.

Let us, then, turn to God's prophetic guidance about the end times. There is a great deal that He wants to tell us about these days in which we are beginning to see the glow of the morning star.

2

Waiting with the Right Motivation

I f our goal is truly to understand biblical prophecy, then our first step will be preparation of our hearts. We must have the right attitude as we face the future. In this chapter, I will provide an objective biblical basis for developing an attitude that honors Jesus and prepares us for His return.

Anticipating His Coming

The first point is basic. It is, in fact, so simple we may not see its importance at first glance. As Christians we are waiting for Jesus Christ; conversely, we are not waiting for the Antichrist.

The Bible teaches that there have been many antichrists, and as we draw near to the close of this age, there are going to be more antichrists. The Bible speaks of one particular character in human history who will be the Antichrist. It is possible that his shadow has already fallen across the stage of human history, and that his appearing is very near at hand. But we are not waiting for him.

I have met fellow believers who are so busy with theories about the Antichrist—his number, his name, the countries he will rule, the methods he will use, how he will put his stamp on people's foreheads and hands—that they are almost advertising agents for him. Our business as Christians is not to be witnesses to the Antichrist but to the Christ. Jesus said, "You shall be witnesses to Me" (Acts 1:8).

Let me provide some Scriptures that make this clear. In 1 Thessalonians Paul congratulates his converts and disciples in Thessalonica, reporting that the people around them are impressed by their way of living:

> They tell how you turned to God from idols to serve the living and true God, and to wait for his Son from heaven, whom he raised from the dead—Jesus, who rescues us from the coming wrath.
>
> 1 Thessalonians 1:9–10, NIV

As Christians we are waiting for the Son of God—Jesus—to return from heaven. Those who are waiting for Him have the guarantee that He rescues us from the coming wrath on the earth—that is, from the Tribulation. How He is going to rescue us is another matter, but I believe that guarantee is given only to those who are clearly waiting for Jesus.

Another Scripture says the same thing:

19

> Just as man is destined to die once, and after that to face judgment, so Christ was sacrificed once to take away the sins of many people; and he will appear a second time, not to bear sin, but to bring salvation to those who are waiting for him.
>
> Hebrews 9:27–28, NIV

When Jesus comes back, He is going to come with salvation only for those who are waiting for Him. Those who are not waiting for Him will encounter His judgment. It is of the greatest personal importance for each of us to so cultivate this attitude of waiting for Jesus that we do not let our attention get distracted by anything else.

Radiant Confidence

One practical result of waiting for Jesus—having our eyes turned toward Him with expectancy—is what I call "radiant confidence." In two beautiful verses from Psalm 34, the psalmist David says: "I sought the LORD, and he answered me; he delivered me from all my fears. Those who look to him are radiant; their faces are never covered with shame" (Psalm 34:4–5, NIV).

These verses are partly David's personal testimony and partly a general statement. First, David is saying, "I could be afraid about what the future holds, but I sought the Lord and He delivered me from all my fears." We need to ask ourselves: Have we sought the Lord and been delivered from all our fears about the future? If not, we can.

Then David goes on with the general statement about having an expectant attitude toward the Lord. Radiance is a practical outworking of looking for the Lord, of waiting for the Lord. The look on our faces tells what direction we are facing. If our faces are dark and overshadowed with care and fear, we are not looking at the light. But if our faces are radiant, peaceful and full of confidence, there is only one explanation: We have our eyes turned toward the source of light—Jesus.

Holy Living

Another important practical result in our lives of the attitude of waiting for Christ is motivation to holy living. This truth is stated many times in the New Testament, for example in the first epistle of John:

> Dear friends, now we are children of God, and what we will be has not yet been made known. But we know that when he appears, we shall be like him, for we shall see him as he is. Everyone who has this hope in him purifies himself, just as he is pure.

> 1 John 3:2–3, NIV

When we have that continual expectancy, the joyful hope that we are going to see the Lord and be transformed to be like Him, the natural, logical application in our lives is that we purify ourselves and make ourselves ready. That standard of purity is a high standard: We purify ourselves just as He, Jesus, is pure.

This kind of waiting motivates both those who minister the Gospel and those being ministered to. Paul declares this in his ministry to the Christians in Thessalonica: "For what is our hope, our joy, or the crown in which we will glory in the presence of our Lord Jesus when he comes? Is it not you? Indeed, you are our glory and joy" (1 Thessalonians 2:19–20, NIV).

Paul seems always to be thinking about the day when he will stand before Jesus and answer for his life and ministry. He explains, "The thing that will make me most proud and joyful is the people I have helped to find their way to Jesus. They are going to be my crown, my glory and my joy." That is true motivation!

Later in the same epistle, as Paul speaks to those to whom he has ministered, he offers one of the most beautiful prayers found anywhere in the Bible: "May he [God] strengthen your hearts so that you will be blameless and holy in the presence of our God and Father when our Lord Jesus comes with all his holy ones" (1 Thessalonians 3:13, NIV).

That is anticipation! Not only does Paul anticipate the coming of the Lord for himself, hoping to offer the Lord a tribute from his life's work, but he also wants those who have come to the Lord through his ministry to have the same attitude of expectancy. Paul knows that attitude will motivate them to become blameless and holy.

Believe me, friend, there is nothing that purifies our lives more effectively than the hope of seeing Jesus. If we really live in that hope, it will have a radical, permanent effect on the way we live. One of my favorite verses illustrates this fact: "The path of the righteous is like the first gleam of dawn, shining ever brighter till the full light of day" (Proverbs 4:18, NIV). When we first come to the Lord and step onto that path, it is like the first gleam of dawn. But as we walk forward continually in that path with that attitude of expectancy, the path becomes ever brighter and brighter until we get to the full glory of midday, the full light of day. That is how the Christian life should be when we are directed toward Jesus and waiting for His return.

Christ Reigns Now and Forever

The next main factor in waiting with the right motivation is centered in the realization that Christ already reigns as King of the universe. Furthermore, He will continue to reign forever. From now until eternity there will never be a time when Christ is not on the throne of the universe.

In the first chapter of Ephesians, Paul is opening the eyes of Christians to the tremendous, immeasurable power of God. In verse 19, he states that God's "incomparably great power [is] for us who believe" (NIV). Then he gives us the standard to measure the power of God available to us as believers in our lives: "That power is like the working of his mighty strength, which he exerted in Christ when he raised him from the dead and seated him at his right hand in the heavenly realms" (Ephesians 1:19–20, NIV).

The same power that raised the dead body of Jesus from the tomb and exalted Him to the highest place in heaven is available to us as believers. Paul then goes on to depict the level of authority to which God has raised Jesus: "[God] seated him at his right hand in the heavenly realms, far above all rule and authority, power and dominion, and every title that can be given, not only in the present age but also in the one to come" (verses 20–21, NIV).

Christ is far above all other forms of rule or authority or power in the whole universe. He is not merely above them—He is *far* above them. He is above all rulers on the natural, human plane: kings, presidents, dictators or whatever

23

other titles they may have. One of His titles is Lord of lords and King of kings. I interpret that this way: He is the Ruler of all rulers and the Governor over all governors.

He is also above all spiritual rulers and authorities in the unseen realm. The Bible reveals that certain unseen powers in the spiritual realm are evil and under Satan's control. In many places the New Testament speaks of "principalities and powers" or "rulers and authorities" with reference to the kind of power and authority Satan would seek to exercise against God's people and God's purposes. Though these are real and we have to reckon with them, we must continually bear in mind that the power and authority bestowed by God upon Jesus is on a far higher level. He is above *all*.

Paul gives us this good news: "God placed all things under his feet and appointed him to be head over everything for the church" (verse 22, NIV).

Those last three words are tremendously important: *for the church*. Jesus is seated in heaven on our account—to represent us, to watch over us, to ensure that God's purposes and promises for us are worked out unfailingly. No human or satanic opposition or hindrance can ever frustrate the promises and the purposes of God on our behalf. Jesus is the head over everything for His Church. How important to realize that! The Church is the primary object of His care and concern. All His power and all His authority are exercised on our behalf.

Furthermore, not only is He seated in heaven, but He is going to remain there from now on and forever. Speaking about Jesus reigning, the Bible says: "For he must reign until he has put all his enemies under his feet" (1 Corinthians 15:25, NIV).

Some people who are preoccupied with the Antichrist and the Great Tribulation actually believe there will be a gap somewhere in the future in human history when Jesus will no longer be reigning. That is not true. He is reigning now, and He will continue to reign until He has put all His enemies under His feet. No matter what happens on earth, Jesus is never going to abdicate that throne to which the Father has raised Him.

And that is not all. Not only has Jesus been exalted above all other forms of authority and power by the Father, but the revelation of Scripture takes us one important step further: Christ shares His authority with His people. This concept is unfolded by Paul:

> But because of his great love for us, God, who is rich in mercy, made us alive with Christ even when we were dead in transgressions—it is by grace you have been saved. And God raised us up with Christ and seated us with him in the heavenly realms in Christ Jesus, in order that in the coming ages he might show the incomparable riches of his grace, expressed in his kindness to us in Christ Jesus.
>
> Ephesians 2:4–7, NIV

In these verses, Paul states three objective, historical facts based upon our relationship through faith with Jesus Christ and our identification with Him. Because we have committed our lives to Jesus and made ourselves one with Him by faith, we are identified in everything God did for Him from His crucifixion onward. Paul specifies three actions God took for Christ that He has also done for us who are "in Christ." In verse 5, Paul says, God "made us alive with Christ." In verse 6, Paul says, "God raised us up [resurrected us] with Christ." Then he goes on to say in the same verse that "God . . . seated us with him in the heavenly realms in Christ Jesus" (NIV).

God has identified us with Christ in these three respects: He has made us alive with Christ, He has raised us up with Christ (resurrected us) and He has seated us with Him in the heavenly realms in Christ Jesus. Jesus is seated on a throne, and when we are seated with Him, we are enthroned with Him. Where He is, we are. Just as He is seated far above all authority and power, we are seated with Him far above all authority and power. Just as He rules, we rule with Him—not in the future, but now.

The same truth of sharing the throne with Christ is stated by Paul in Romans:

> For if, by the trespass of the one man, death reigned through that one man, how much more will those who receive God's abundant provision of grace and of the gift of righteousness reign in life through the one man, Jesus Christ.
>
> Romans 5:17, NIV

When we are identified with Jesus Christ, we reign with Him in life. Just as He reigns, we reign with Him. Just as He is on the throne, we share the throne with Him. This is important for us to realize as we go into the future.

Continuous Victory Is Ours

Let's take these truths one important step further. Christ exercises His authority through His believing people and makes continuous victory possible for us. We see this in the first two verses of Psalm 110, quoted in the New Testament more often than any other passage from the Old Testament. Jesus Himself quoted these verses. The psalmist says:

> The LORD says to my Lord: "Sit at My right hand, until I make Thine enemies a footstool for Thy feet." The LORD will stretch forth Thy strong scepter from Zion, saying, "Rule in the midst of Thine enemies."
>
> Psalm 110:1–2, NASB

From the lips of Jesus Himself, we know the application of the first verse. *The* LORD is God the Father. *My Lord*, that is, David's Lord, is the Messiah. So God the Father said to Jesus Christ the Messiah after His death and resurrection, "Sit at My right hand, until I make Thine enemies a footstool for Thy feet." We have seen that this has already been fulfilled. Jesus is already at God's right hand. He is waiting for God to put all His enemies finally under His feet, but He is already ruling.

Verse 2 of Psalm 110 goes on to say: "The LORD will stretch forth Thy strong scepter from Zion, saying, 'Rule in the midst of Thine enemies.'" In Hebrew, *Thy strong scepter* is literally "the scepter of Thy strength." A scepter was the mark of a ruler in Old Testament culture and history. There is an example of this in God's dealings with Moses, Aaron and the princes of the tribes of Israel. Each prince was directed to engrave his name on his rod or scepter. The rod of the man whom God had chosen to be the prince and ruler, the high priest, was the rod that blossomed, budded and brought forth almonds in 24 hours. The other rods remained unchanged. (See Numbers 17.) The rod or the scepter was the mark of a ruler's authority. Having the name

27

of the ruler on it meant that that authority could never be transferred to another. It was marked with the name of the one to whom it belonged.

Zion in the Bible means "the assembly of God's people met in divine order." Out of the assembly of God's people, the Lord stretches forth the authority of Jesus, which is in His name, and rules over the nation. I believe that the Lord who stretches forth that scepter is God the Holy Spirit. So we have all three Persons of the Godhead present there: God the Father raised God the Son to sit with Him on the throne, and then God the Holy Spirit, through the assembly of God's people (through their proclamations, their preaching, their prayers and their testimony), stretches forth the rod of Christ's authority over the earth. In this way, Christ, through His people, now rules in the midst of His enemies.

It is important that we see two truths here about this rulership: Christ is ruling, but there are enemies on every hand. Some people have the impression Christ will be ruling only when there are no more enemies, but that is not true. This is the critical period in God's dealings with the human race—*when Christ is already ruling but the enemies are not fully subdued.* We have to balance the two facts. Of course there are many enemies. They are active, vocal and vicious. But Christ is ruling in the midst of His enemies, exercising His authority through us, His people, as we learn how to use the authority that is in His name.

Furthermore, Christ sends us out as His representatives to exercise His authority on His behalf. This is the final commission of Jesus to His disciples at the end of Matthew's gospel:

28

Then Jesus came to them and said, "All authority in heaven and on earth has been given to me. Therefore go and make disciples of all nations, baptizing them in the name of the Father and of the Son and of the Holy Spirit, and teaching them to obey everything I have commanded you. And surely I am with you always, to the very end of the age."

Matthew 28:18–20, NIV

What is the connection between the authority and the going? The authority has been given to Jesus, but it is our responsibility to exercise that authority. We accomplish this, in His name, by going and doing what He has commissioned us to go and do. As we obey His commission, He says, "I'm with you always, right to the end of the present age. If you have any hindrances or obstacles, remember, just appeal to Me. I'm on the throne. I'm there for your benefit, and I'll see to it that you can do what I have commissioned you to do."

That is the picture: Christ is on the throne. He is ruling, but He is exercising the authority that is in His name through His people as we obey Him. That will continue right to the end of the present age.

The Triumphal Procession

Let's look at this truth of Christ's victory manifested through us from another angle. About the death and resurrection of Jesus, Paul says: "Having disarmed the powers and authorities, he made a public spectacle of them, triumphing over them by the cross" (Colossians 2:15, NIV).

The "spectacle" Paul speaks of here refers not to winning a victory, but the celebration of a victory that has already

29

been won. This was a custom during the days of the Roman Empire. If a Roman general had been victorious in a campaign that added territory to the Roman Empire, the Senate of Rome voted him a triumph when he came home. They placed him in a chariot drawn by two white horses. The chariot was then led through the city streets, which were lined with applauding citizens. Behind the chariot came the prisoners of war—the people whom the general had conquered—as evidence of his victory.

When Jesus died on the cross and rose from the dead, He triumphed over all satanic opposition—all satanic authorities and powers that resist the purposes of God and God's people. He led them behind His chariot in public display and the whole, unseen universe applauded His victory.

But it does not end there. In 2 Corinthians Paul goes on to say: "Thanks be to God, who always leads us in triumphal procession in Christ and through us spreads everywhere the fragrance of the knowledge of him" (2 Corinthians 2:14, NIV). Not only is Jesus moving in triumphal procession, but He has called us up to ride in the chariot with Him! We share not only His victory but His triumph, the celebration of His victory. We are identified with Him. We are not there on the sidewalk applauding. We are certainly not among the captives that are being led behind Him in chains. We are riding in the place of honor with the Victor.

As we share His triumph, something beautiful and wonderful happens: God, through us, spreads everywhere the fragrance of the knowledge of Him. There is a kind of fragrance that comes out of our victorious living, and it permeates the atmosphere where we live. Even people who do not understand the Gospel or do not appreciate theology are aware of our victorious living.

Notice two final points about this victory: One, God *always* leads us in triumph; and, two, through us He spreads *everywhere* the fragrance of the knowledge of Him. When we put together those two words, *always* and *everywhere*, we realize that in every time and in every place total victory is possible for us as the people of God. This happens if, by faith, we learn how to share Jesus' victory and His public triumph. Is that not glorious?

As a brief recap, here are three basic principles for a right attitude toward the future:

We are waiting for Christ, not for the Antichrist.

Christ already reigns and will continue to reign.

Christ exercises His authority through us always and everywhere.

When we grasp those facts, we are going to face the future with strong confidence because our hearts are ready.

3

Seven Principles of Biblical Prophecy

Thus far we understand that the attitude with which we approach the challenges of a changing world has a great deal to do with how we experience those challenges. Our outlook will largely determine our position as the future unfolds. So we have a choice to make. Will we be optimistic or pessimistic? To use a familiar illustration, will we decide to see the glass as half-full or half-empty? Is the glass on its way to being filled or is it showing signs of being drained?

The Bible gives us solid, objective grounds for facing the future as optimists rather than as pessimists. As we look at the world around us in the light of the Bible, we can say, "The glass of history is half-full, not half-empty." In other words, the purposes of God, clearly predicted in the Bible, have been fulfilled up to this present date in time and history. We can, therefore, be confident any plans not yet accomplished will be.

This is generally not the approach people take. Many who look upon the human situation today are pessimistic. They say, "Time is running out. The atmosphere is being polluted. Resources are being exhausted. A population explosion is upon us. We're not going to have enough food." This is really saying, "The glass is being drained." From my point of view, however, as a student and believer of the Bible, when I look at the world scene today, I can praise the Lord and say, "The glass is being filled. God's purposes have been worked out to this point, and they will continue to be worked out—come what may!"

Let's embrace that optimistic attitude as our foundation as we explore seven recommendations for understanding biblical prophecy.

1. Some Prophecies Will Remain Secret

The book of Deuteronomy contains two great, basic principles for understanding and applying prophecy, articulated by Moses to the children of Israel: "The secret things belong to the LORD our God, but those things which are revealed belong to us and to our children forever, that we may do all the words of this law" (Deuteronomy 29:29).

God has secrets He does not permit us to know. They belong to Him and are simply not our business. Additionally, however, there are truths God has chosen to reveal to us. These belong to us. And in regard to what God has shown to us, we are responsible to act on it, to obey it, to let it have impact on our lives according to God's plan for us.

One common mistake in looking to the future is to become so intrigued with the secret things that we fail to obey the revealed things. Here is a clear warning for us. Anyone who claims to be able to reveal the secret things is really a false prophet—one who has, by his own lips, identified himself. People who do not understand the nature of biblical prophecy will be deceived by such a person. We have to resist the temptation to try to figure out God's secret things, recognizing that if God wants to keep something secret, it is futile to waste time trying to find it out! For those who focus on finding out the secret things of God, the result will be frustration, confusion and disappointment.

Let's take two examples of predictions from the New Testament that illustrate revealed things and secret things. First, an example of something that God has revealed: the words spoken by the angels to the apostles as they stood on the Mount of Olives looking upward after Jesus had been taken up to heaven: "This same Jesus, who has been taken from you into heaven, will come back in the same way you have seen him go into heaven" (Acts 1:11, NIV). This is a revealed truth—something we all need to know, which should affect our lives in numerous ways.

Next, let's look at a secret thing, something that God has not made known and that we have no right to try to know, as stated by Jesus Himself in the gospel of Mark. Speaking of events and various signs of the close of the age and His personal return to earth, Jesus says: "No one knows about that day or hour, not even the angels in heaven, nor the Son, but only the Father" (Mark 13:32, NIV).

The precise day and hour of the return of Jesus to earth is unknowable to anyone in the universe except God the Father. Even Jesus, the Son of God, does not know when He will return but is awaiting the Father's signal. If someone declares that he can determine the day and the hour of Jesus' return, we know he is not agreeing with the Bible.

This is why, in the verses that follow His statement, Jesus admonishes the disciples and us with a parable:

> "Be on guard! Be alert! You do not know when that time will come. It's like a man going away: He leaves his house and puts his servants in charge, each with his assigned task, and tells the one at the door to keep watch. Therefore keep watch because you do not know when the owner of the house will come back—whether in the evening, or at midnight, or when the rooster crows, or at dawn. If he comes suddenly, do not let him find you sleeping. What I say to you, I say to everyone: 'Watch!'"
>
> Mark 13:33–37, NIV

In this story the master left his servants behind, each with an assigned task—something specific to accomplish during his absence. The assignment of the man at the door, for example, was to watch for the master's return.

This is true of us as Christians. Here on earth we each have assigned tasks—jobs we are responsible to do and for which we will be answerable to God when we stand before the judgment seat of Christ. We must not become so preoccupied with the secret things, such as the exact day and hour of the Lord's return, that we neglect the revealed things, such as our assigned tasks.

2. Prophecy Is Given for a Reason

Deuteronomy 29 reminds us that truths are shown to us "that we may do [them]" (verse 29). The purpose of biblical prophecy is not just to make us wiser than our neighbors or let us know what is coming next. Its purpose is to give us things to do. My experience with God has been that if we obey what He reveals, He reveals more. If we do not obey what He reveals, He does not reveal more. Why should He? He says, "Carry on. Do what I've told you to do, and I'll show you the next thing."

In 1958 I was in Kenya, East Africa, serving as the principal of a training college for African teachers. One morning I drove my little car seven miles into the main city, Kisumu, to have it serviced. I had an extensive "to do" list to take care of in town—a very busy day. As I walked out of the service station after leaving my car, however, God said to me, *Not only does your car need service, you need service, too.* I realized I needed "oiling" and "greasing" desperately as well. So I gave up my whole schedule and walked about ten minutes down to the shore of Lake Victoria Nyanza, the second largest inland lake in the world. It is a beautiful and tranquil place, and I sat down on a bench under some large, overarching trees, pulled out my pocket New Testament and flipped it open. I was not looking for any Scripture in particular.

My eyes fell on Matthew 24:14: "This gospel of the kingdom will be preached in all the world as a witness to all the nations, and then the end will come." At that moment, God made it clear to me: *This is priority number one for My people.*

In my ministry as principal, my primary aim was to win my students to the Lord. I was not by any means in a backslidden state. In fact, I was clearly in the will of God. Rarely did any student leave that college after five years without becoming saved and baptized in the Holy Spirit, so I certainly was not wasting my time there. But I sensed the Lord speaking to me of something more important, and I responded to Him. "Lord, if I'm not yet fully identified with Your primary purpose, I want to be. Will You arrange it?"

It took about twenty years for the Lord to bring me fully into alignment with His purpose, but in 1978 (the year I married Ruth) I began a totally new phase of my ministry with the start of a radio program. I had never been interested in radio ministry, but, in faith, I started broadcasting on eight stations in the United States. We had a monthly budget of eight thousand dollars—and no idea where the money would come from. Today, that program, in more than a dozen languages, is heard virtually around the world every day. It is broadcast at least once every 24 hours into China.

I had no idea the radio program would ever air outside the United States or be heard in any language other than English. But God did it! He began to line me up with His primary purpose—that "this gospel of the kingdom will be preached in all the world as a witness to all the nations, and then the end will come."

Since then I have been privileged to minister in large Bible teaching conferences in all sorts of improbable places, such as Turkey or Moscow or Almaty, the capital city of Kazakhstan, one of the southern provinces of the former Soviet empire. That verse became the focus of my life. But it did not all happen in a day; God had to work it out gradually. Let me emphasize the point again: If I had not obeyed what God showed me that day from Matthew 24:14, I doubt that God would have ever shown me anything else. *Revelation is conditional upon obedience.* If we do not obey, God will not show us anything more.

3. Prophecy Is Given for a Specific Time and Situation

Many prophecies relate to a specific time and situation, and, prior to that point, we may not be able to understand what they all mean. In Jeremiah 30, for instance, we have a specific prophecy concerning the restoration of Israel to her own land. (I would add that most biblical prophecies concerning the end times assume the presence of Israel as a nation in her own land. We will discuss Israel more extensively in chapters that follow.) Thus, these prophecies could not be fulfilled until the State of Israel was restored. Many years ago, a dear respected brother in the Lord made this erroneous statement: "The restoration of the State of Israel could not be from God—because if it were from God it would have produced peace." If he had been familiar with biblical prophecy, which says exactly the opposite, he would not have said that. We see this in the following passages.

> "'For behold, the days are coming,' says the LORD, 'that I will bring back from captivity [exile] My people Israel and Judah,' says the LORD. 'And I will cause them to return to the land that I gave to their fathers, and they shall possess it.'"
>
> Jeremiah 30:3

Anyone acquainted with the Bible knows where the land is that God gave to these fathers. There is only one place answering that description: It is a little strip of territory at the east end of the Mediterranean. Continuing in Jeremiah, we read:

> Now these are the words that the LORD spoke concerning Israel and Judah. "For thus says the LORD: 'We have heard

a voice of trembling, of fear, and not of peace. Ask now, and see, whether a man is ever in labor with child? So why do I see every man with his hands on his loins like a woman in labor, and all faces turned pale? Alas! For that day is great, so that none is like it; and it is the time of Jacob's trouble, but he shall be saved out of it.'"

Jeremiah 30:4–7

Far from predicting peace when Israel is restored to her territory, the Bible warns us there will be a time of tribulation and anguish without parallel in Jewish history. And considering Jewish history, that is a startling statement. The Lord says concerning this time not that His people "will be saved from it" but that they "will be saved *out* of it." That statement applies to many situations in our lives today. God does not always save us *from* things, but He saves us *out* of things. He lets us get into them, and then He saves us out of them.

At the end of this chapter, in verse 24, is a kind of postscript: "In the latter days you will consider it." In other words, "You really will not have any use for this prophecy until the time of the end." I would say it is exceedingly meaningful today, because we see these Scriptures being proved right in front of our eyes. Likewise, many prophecies are understood only when the appropriate moment arrives.

4. Prophecy Is Given for Guidance

Another main purpose of biblical prophecy is to guide us in what we are to do and what we are not to do. It is directive. People who do not know biblical prophecy may try to do what can never come to pass, simply because God has said it will never happen. If God has declared a matter will not happen, it is a waste of time to pray that it will happen or try to make it happen.

One example comes from Matthew 24:19–20, verses that apply to the situation after the Jews have been returned to their land. Jesus says: "But woe to those who are pregnant and to those who are nursing babies in those days! And pray that your flight may not be in winter or on the Sabbath."

Any of us living in that land might be inclined to pray, "God, don't let us have to flee," but that is a useless prayer. We *are* going to have to flee, so we should pray within the parameters He gives us. Jesus says that even though we will have to flee, pray that it will not be in winter. Why? Because survival can be tough in winter, especially for pregnant women or women with nursing babies. And He said to pray also that it may not be on the Sabbath. Why would we pray that? First of all, that has no meaning at all unless there is a Jewish state. I lived in Israel—then called Palestine—while it was still under the British mandate, and the Sabbath was no different from any other day. But now that it is a Jewish state, there is no public transportation on the Sabbath. The majority of people do not go anywhere. A large group of people fleeing on the Sabbath day would be extremely conspicuous.

As we will see, this is just one example of many prophetic Scriptures that tell us what is going to happen in the future. If God says something will take place, it is a waste of time to pray it will not happen. We may, however, discern the parameters of revealed prophecy and pray toward that end.

5. The Spirit of Prophecy Focuses on Jesus

Number five is in a different category. We find this principle in Revelation 19:10: "For the testimony of Jesus is the spirit of prophecy."

Scripture is talking here about the spirit of prophecy, not just the words of prophecy. It says that biblical prophecy always focuses on the Lord Jesus; He is the central theme of all biblical prophecy from Genesis to Revelation. Jesus says:

> "When He, the Spirit of truth, has come, He will guide you into all truth; for He will not speak on His own authority, but whatever He hears He will speak; and He will tell you things to come. He will glorify Me, for He will take of what is Mine and declare it to you."
>
> John 16:13–14

This is the acid test of any manifestation to determine whether or not it is of the Holy Spirit: If it is of the Holy Spirit, it will glorify Jesus. It will focus our attention on Jesus. It will show us something about Jesus we never saw before.

Prophecies that glorify humans are not from the Holy Spirit. In fact, if the Holy Spirit begins to move and human personalities slip in and take center stage, the Holy Spirit will politely withdraw. He has done that a number of times in the last hundred years. Many moves of the Holy Spirit were quenched because people wanted the focus on themselves. Any true prophetic revelation will always glorify Jesus.

6. Prophecy Means What It Says

If a prophecy is given as a literal word, we must take care not to "spiritualize" it. Consider the many prophecies about the first coming of Jesus. Every one of them was fulfilled literally, as we noted in the first chapter. Jesus was born of a literal virgin, not a metaphorical virgin. He was born in Bethlehem, literally. He was called out of Egypt, literally. He healed the sick, literally. He was crucified, literally; there was nothing spiritual or metaphorical about it. He was buried, literally, and, thank God, He rose again from the dead, literally. He ascended into heaven, literally. Every prophecy concerning the first appearance of Jesus has been fulfilled literally. There is no precedent for making literal prophecy allegorical or interpreting it in some way other than the plain, natural meaning of the words.

Some prophecies, however, *are* allegorical, and it is legitimate to interpret them allegorically. Nobody supposes, for instance, that the king of Greece was a goat or that the king of Persia was a ram (see Daniel 8). We know those images are allegorical. But where the Scripture does not warrant an allegorical interpretation, it is a mistake to make it allegorical.

As we face the tremendous pressures and dangers of this latter time, the prophecies concerning this period are going to be fulfilled with frightening literalness. Things really are going to move out of their places. Things really are going to fall from heaven. There are going to be more and more real, literal earthquakes.

I would like to mention in this regard that Israel is Israel. That is simple and basic. Israel is not the Church, and the Church is not Israel. If you want a little study on that subject, I wrote a book in which I point out 79 Scriptures in the New Testament that mention the word *Israel*, none of which applies to the Church (*The Destiny of Israel and the Church*, © 2007, Derek Prince Ministries–International). We must be careful not to be super-spiritual in our interpretation of prophecy. Prophecy means what it says.

7. God Has Total Sovereignty

For this final principle, we must bear in mind a point I made earlier. It is vital to our progress so I want to repeat it here: God has total sovereignty and supremacy, and He is totally just. We can be sure as we look at end time prophecies that He has never said anything that is not true. And He has never made a mistake in our lives. We may think He has, but He has not. He is absolutely righteous.

So these are the seven principles that I want to put before us as we study biblical prophecy:

There are secret things and there are revealed things. Never waste time trying to find out the secret things, but be sure to obey the revealed things.

God reveals things that we may do them. And if we do not do them, He will not reveal any more to us.

Some prophecies are given for a specific time and will not be understood until the time comes.

Prophecy is given very often to keep us from wrong action and wrong prayer. If God has said something will happen, it will happen. If God has said something will not happen, it will not happen. If we want to pray sensible, effective prayers, we need to know the parameters of the will of God as revealed in prophecy.

The spirit of prophecy is the revelation of Jesus. All true prophecy given by the Holy Spirit ultimately has one theme: Jesus.

Prophetic words should be given their plain meaning.

We must always acknowledge and bow before God's total sovereignty. I do not read the Bible in order to correct God's ethics. A lot of people do. A lot of people have the idea that God is doing something unjust in the Middle East at the moment, but He is not. God is always right.

4

The "Spine" of Biblical Prophecy

When I was fairly young in my faith, I heard a statement by a Jewish believer that I never forgot. Myer Pearlman was a member of the General Council of the Assemblies of God in the United States at the time. This is what he said: Interpreting prophecy is just like putting together the pieces of a human skeleton. If we want to do it successfully, we have to start with the right piece—and the right piece is the spine. When we get the spine in place, we can begin to fit the other members onto it. In this chapter and several chapters that follow, we will start fitting the pieces of biblical prophecy together, attaching them to the spine as defined by Myer Pearlman: Jesus' discourse on the Mount of Olives, recorded in Matthew 24–25.

Sometimes we tend to overlook the fact that Jesus was a prophet. The people of His time acknowledged Him as a prophet even if they did not acknowledge Him as the Son of God. He was the greatest of all the great Hebrew prophets, and His greatest prophetic discourse is found in these two chapters. In spite of the chapter division, there is no division in the discourse. The first part of the discourse is also found in Mark 13 and Luke 21. These are three different perspectives of the same discourse, almost like three television cameras all focused on Jesus. Each records what He says and does, yet from a slightly different perspective. To get the full picture we need to put all three together.

Matthew 24 records that Jesus gives this discourse while on the western slope of the Mount of Olives with His closest disciples. He was apparently seated there looking out over the city of Jerusalem and the Temple area, a position I have had the delight of occupying many times in my life.

The stage had actually been set earlier: "Then Jesus went out and departed from the temple, and His disciples came up to show Him the buildings of the temple" (Matthew 24:1). King Herod had just spent 46 years renovating, extending and glorifying that Temple. It was considered to be one of the wonders of the ancient world. It was also the center and focus of the entire national and religious life of the Jewish people. It was their great pride and joy. That is why Jesus' response to His disciples' pleasure in showing Him the Temple buildings would have been almost like a blow to the solar plexus for them. "And Jesus said to them, 'Do you not see all these things? Assuredly, I say to you, not one stone shall be left here upon another, that shall not be thrown down'" (verse 2).

We cannot possibly understand the impact of those words. Thus, as soon as the disciples have an opportunity—after Jesus leaves the Temple area, crosses the brook Kidron and walks up the western slope of the Mount of Olives—they get alone with Jesus and question Him. The next verse says: "Now as He sat on the Mount of Olives, the disciples came to Him privately, saying, 'Tell us, when will these things be? And what will be the sign of Your coming, and of the end of the age?'" (verse 3).

The disciples obviously believe that if the Temple were destroyed, such a disaster would mark the end of the age. They cannot imagine that the age would continue if the Temple were destroyed. The disciples think they are asking Jesus one question, but actually they are asking two. The first is "When will these things be?" This refers to the destruction of the Temple and Jerusalem. The second is "What will be the sign of Your coming and of the end of the age?" Jesus answers both questions.

The First Question: The Temple

I want to note here the answer to the first question as recorded in Luke 21.

> "But when you see Jerusalem surrounded by armies, then know that its desolation is near. Then let those who are in Judea flee to the mountains, let those who are in the midst of her depart, and let not those who are in the country enter her. For these are the days of vengeance, that all things which are written may be fulfilled. But woe to those who are pregnant and to those who are nursing babies in those days! For there will be great distress in the land and wrath upon this people.

And they will fall by the edge of the sword, and be led away captive into all nations. And Jerusalem will be trampled by Gentiles until the times of the Gentiles are fulfilled."

Luke 21:20–24

That is the answer to the question "When will these things happen? When will the Temple be destroyed and Jerusalem be destroyed?" Jesus says, "This is the sign: When you see Jerusalem surrounded by armies, know that its desolation is near." This was fulfilled historically in A.D. 70. The Roman commander Vespasian laid siege to Jerusalem and surrounded it with his armies. He received word from Rome that he had been chosen as the next emperor, which necessitated his return to Rome to receive his position. Vespasian lifted the siege of Jerusalem temporarily and the armies withdrew— but only temporarily.

Those Jews in Jerusalem who acknowledged Jesus as a prophet of the Lord understood the application of these words. They fled from Jerusalem to a town called Pella on the east side of the Jordan. Vespasian's successor, Titus, re-formed the siege, gathered the armies together and continued to besiege Jerusalem until the words of Jesus had been exactly fulfilled. The whole city was destroyed. The Temple was destroyed so completely that not one single stone was left upon another. In the course of that war, two million Jews were killed and one million were sold into captivity as slaves throughout the Roman Empire. At one point, in fact, there was such a glut of slaves in the markets that even at low prices no one was buying them.

These words of Jesus were fulfilled, and note this: The people who gave heed to what Jesus prophesied saved their lives. (This is a very important lesson.) Here again are Jesus' words to His disciples:

> "For there will be great distress in the land [the land of Israel] and wrath upon this people [the Jewish people]. And they will fall by the edge of the sword, and be led away captive into all nations. And Jerusalem will be trampled by Gentiles until the times of the Gentiles are fulfilled."
>
> Luke 21:23–24

The "times of the Gentiles" are times when Gentile powers rule the land given by God eternally to Israel. That second half of verse 24 covers nearly two thousand years.

One of the key years in Jewish history is 1967, marking the Six-Day War. At that time, for the first time in nearly two thousand years, the Jewish people regained control of that vital area called the Old City. But the prophecy has not yet been fulfilled completely, because the Jewish people did not take control. They could have done so, but they did not, and so the Temple area is still occupied by a Muslim mosque. It is as if we are right on the verge, but we have not actually stepped into position because Jerusalem has not been liberated from Gentile domination.

Then Jesus goes on immediately to say:

> "And there will be signs in the sun, in the moon, and in the stars; and on the earth distress of nations, with perplexity, the sea and the waves roaring; men's hearts failing them from fear and the expectation of those things which are coming on the earth, for the powers of the heavens will be shaken. Then they will see the Son of Man coming in a cloud with power and great glory."
>
> Luke 21:25–27

When Jerusalem is finally liberated from Gentile domination, the events on the calendar move swiftly to the return of Jesus in person.

The Second Question and a Warning

Now we go to Matthew 24 to consider the disciples' second question: "What will be the sign of Your coming, and of the end of the age?" Notice the disciples do not say "the signs [plural]" but "the sign [singular] of Your coming." Jesus answers that question, but He does not answer it immediately. He leads up to His answer. Let's follow His line of thought.

Jesus begins His analysis of the closing phase of this age with a word of warning: "Take heed that no one deceives you. For many will come in My name, saying, 'I am the Christ [the Messiah],' and will deceive many" (Matthew 24:4–5).

The first great warning given to us concerning the period of the end is a warning against deception by false messiahs, which is repeated twice in the course of this prophecy. Three times in connection with the close of the age Jesus warns His disciples against being deceived. In my opinion, deception is the greatest single danger that threatens us as Christians— greater than persecution, greater than war.

I have heard people say, "Well, it could never happen to me!" I want to warn you: If you think it never will happen to you, it *will* happen to you. That statement is a sure mark you are already under deception. Jesus warns His own disciples, who have been close to Him for three and a half years, who have heard all His teachings and seen all His miracles: "Be careful; don't come under deception."

We have only one sure guarantee against deception, given to us in 2 Thessalonians 2:10: "Receive the love of the truth." Our only protection from deception is not something negative, but something positive—the love of the truth. The Greek word used there is *agape*, which is the strongest form of love. To avoid being deceived, we have to have a passionate love for the truth. It is not enough to have a quiet time every morning or attend a good church or say our prayers. We have to have a passionate commitment to the truth of the Word of God to avoid being deceived.

In Matthew 24:5, Jesus says, "For many will come in My name, saying, 'I am the Christ [the Messiah],' and will deceive many." That prophecy by Jesus has been fulfilled. A Jewish encyclopedia lists approximately forty false messiahs who have come to the Jewish people since the time of Jesus, and all have deceived some of the people.

A few of these false messiahs deceived almost the whole nation. Bar Kochba claimed to be the messiah and led the Jewish people in the final revolt against Rome, which was utterly suppressed. The whole nation was either killed or taken into captivity. Moses of Crete led about five thousand Jews out into the sea believing that the Lord would come—and they all drowned. It happened again in the year 1666 when Sabbatai Zevi told the Jewish people he was the messiah, promising to restore them to the land of Israel, and thousands of them gathered there. To save his life he converted to Islam. What a bitter disappointment for all those believers! This is a repeated feature of Jewish history. Jesus is a true prophet: Everything He said has been or will be fulfilled.

Thus far, then, we see that Jesus' prophetic words regarding the destruction of the Temple and the appearing of false messiahs have been fulfilled. Now we are ready to view the main features He offers in His discourse on the Mount of Olives about the signs of the times that are being fulfilled in our day.

As we will see, the first grouping—wars, famines, earthquakes and pestilences—is just the beginning. Yet Jesus gives us His assurance: "When you hear of wars and commotions [or troubles], do not be terrified; for these things must come to pass first, but the end will not come immediately" (Luke 21:9). Let's now continue our piecing together of the "spine" of end time prophecy.

5

The Beginning of Sorrows

As Jesus continues His prophetic discourse, He gives His disciples a sense of the progression of the events of the last days. Matthew records these words: "For nation will rise against nation, and kingdom against kingdom. And there will be famines, pestilences, and earthquakes in various places. All these are the beginning of sorrows" (Matthew 24:7–8).

I want to focus on that word *sorrows* for a moment. Here it means "birth pangs" or "labor pains." When the events Jesus describes in verse 7 happen, the labor pains have begun. We all know what labor pains lead up to—some by experience and some by observation. After labor pains, the next major event will be a birth. That is exactly what is meant here. These labor pains must precede the birth of God's Kingdom on earth.

We also know that the nearer the birth of a baby, the more frequent and more intense the birth pains become until the baby is eventually born. In the same way Jesus says that once these birth pains start in human history, they will become more frequent and more intense. There is no way of reversing that process; the birth will occur.

Here is a question that represents one way we can test ourselves regarding end time prophecy: Do we want to stop the pains or do we want to have the baby? If we want to have the baby, we must have the birth pangs, for there is no way to give birth without them. If we say, "Oh, I can't stand all this! It's too terrible. I don't know why I'm living in this time," then we are not really excited about the baby. But if we want the baby, we will welcome the birth pangs, even if they are very painful.

Let's check ourselves by asking which is more important—the coming of God's Kingdom on earth or not being involved in the birth pangs. We might as well make the right choice, because we will be involved in the birth pangs anyhow.

Here are five features Jesus gives us in this discourse, showing events as the sorrows of the end begin:

1. Wars, famines, earthquakes and pestilences
2. Worldwide persecution of Christians
3. Apostasy and betrayal among Christians
4. False prophets with cults
5. Love growing cold

1. Wars and Natural Disasters

Along with war—international and worldwide—we have in Matthew 24:7–8 three major attacks on the human race: famines, pestilences and earthquakes. Together these represent the beginning of birth pangs of the coming age.

In the world today there are two kinds of wars: political wars and ethnic wars. World War I and World War II were both essentially political wars—wars fought by world powers to establish their dominion.

The word *nation* in Greek is *ethnos*, from which we get the word *ethnic*. Before World War I, which began in 1914, there was an ethnic war of which we are told very little. In 1913 the Turks in the Middle East massacred one million Christian Armenians. That was not a political war; it was an ethnic war—Turks against Armenians. Today ethnic wars are breaking out everywhere. This is a major feature of our time. In the course of one year alone (1993) 34 wars were fought—most of them ethnic wars.

In my lifetime I have lived through two world wars. Today famine is endemic in many areas of the world; probably more than ten million people perish yearly through famine. Wherever famine comes, pestilences almost always follow. There are areas of Southeast Asia where all this is being enacted before our eyes. And the scientific record of earthquakes shows an amazing increase in the frequency and intensity of earthquakes in the last fifty to one hundred years.

2. Hatred Grows toward Christians . . .

I mentioned above that Jesus gives us a sense of progression regarding the last days. This is enhanced by His use of a key word: *then*. This word, which occurs numerous times, indicates a succession of events following one another systematically. That is the nature of this discourse of Jesus—it is systematic, thorough and basic. (See the Appendix for a listing of this systematic occurrence of the word *then*.)

As we look at Matthew 24:9, bearing in mind that we have now entered the period of birth pangs, we see the first of the *then*s: "Then they will deliver you up to tribulation and kill you, and you will be hated by all nations for My name's sake."

I often ask people, "Who is the *you* mentioned there?" The answer is not grammatically correct, but *you* is *us*. Can we absorb this fact? At this point people will deliver us up—Christians, followers of Jesus—to tribulation and kill us. We will be hated by all nations for Jesus' name's sake.

Many people pray for revival, and that includes me. But when the Church experiences revival, it will discover for the first time how much the world really hates it. We need to bear that in mind.

3. . . . And among Christians

Now we look at the next *then*: "And then many will be offended, will betray one another, and will hate one another" (Matthew 24:10). Again, the word *many* refers to Christians. When Scripture speaks of turning away from the faith, it means the Christian faith.

Why will Christians betray one another? To save their own lives. Actually this is not so unusual; it has been happening for years in China and the former Soviet Union and in some Muslim nations. The fact that those of us in the United States have not seen much of it yet does not mean it is not already happening in many parts of the world. I have no doubt that fairly soon it will begin to happen in the United States as well.

So this is the progression: Under the pressure of the persecution Jesus is speaking about, some Christians will renounce their faith and betray their fellow Christians. Hatred will develop between the Christians who remain loyal to Jesus and those who betray Him. And those who betray their fellow Christians will betray them to the secular authorities for judgment. (Here is another *then*.) "Then many false prophets will rise up and deceive many" (verse 11).

4. False Prophets Will Rise

Every cult is the product of a false prophet, and we cannot number the cults that have confronted us in recent years. I hate to say it, but some of those false prophets are not outside the churches but inside the churches. In my study of the life of Jeremiah, I am impressed by the fact that at the close of the history of the people of Judah, there was apparently only one true prophet, Jeremiah. There were, however, countless false prophets. This was an indication that the nation was on the verge of final judgment and disaster. The soothing words of the false prophets who promised peace caused most of the people to ignore the true words of Jeremiah, who said disaster was coming.

Many of us have heard prophets who promise everything except what is really going to happen. If someone predicts something false, he is a false prophet. Under the Law of Moses he would have been put to death. It is safe to say there would be far fewer prophets today if that law still applied!

I believe anyone who is a genuine prophet today must emphasize the word *repent*. The condition of the world and the condition of our churches demand repentance. We can speak entertaining words and nice prophecies about people's futures, but if there is no call for repentance I question whether or not the one who makes such promises is a true prophet.

5. Love Will Grow Cold

Jesus shows us the result of this turning away from the faith: "And because lawlessness will abound, the love of many will grow cold" (Matthew 24:12).

Again, the word *many* refers to Christians. The Greek word for *love* used here is *agape*, the word for Christian love, so this is not talking about the world's brand of love. The love of many Christians will grow cold in this lawlessness. Here is a little saying I coined: "Lawlessness breeds lovelessness." There is so much lawlessness in our culture today that we tend to become hardened. We tend to say, "We can't prevent it; what's the use? Why should I be concerned? I'll just look after myself." America today in particular is under a siege of lawlessness.

How important to see that lawlessness leads to lovelessness! The world has a false idea of love being free and uninhibited— doing whatever one pleases. That is not God's kind of love. God's kind of love requires discipline and self-control. True love is not selfish, aggressive or self-seeking. Only discipline will produce that kind of love in Christians. So lawlessness and the love of God are opposites. Where lawlessness abounds, the love of God is squeezed out of people. We must take the necessary precautions to maintain our love for the Lord and for one another.

Enduring to the End

These, then, are five main features of the beginning of birth pangs Jesus gives in His discourse. Not everyone will give in to fear or persecution or lawlessness. What does Jesus promise for those who remain faithful? "He who endures to the end shall be saved" (Matthew 24:13).

In the original Greek, this phrase is even more precise. It says, "He who has endured to the end shall be saved." Thank God, we are saved now. But if we want to stay saved, we have to endure. There is really only one way to learn endurance: by enduring. Endurance is God's preparation for what lies ahead. We should not complain about it. Scripture says,

> Count it all joy when you fall into various trials, knowing that the testing of your faith produces patience [endurance, NASB]. But let patience have its perfect work, that you may be perfect and complete, lacking nothing.
>
> James 1:2–4

For us to be perfect and complete, we have to let endurance have its perfect work. That is the key to survival.

The Ultimate Sign: The Second Question Answered

So far in this discourse we have seen various *signs* (plural) of the end, but Jesus has not yet answered the disciples' second question, "What will be the one *sign* [singular] of the end of the age?" When we get to Matthew 24:14 we have the answer: "And this gospel of the kingdom will be preached in all the world as a witness to all the nations, and then the end will come."

When will the end come? When this Gospel of the Kingdom has been preached in all the world as a witness to all the nations. This is a very important statement. It means that the real initiative in world history is not with the politicians, the military commanders or the scientists, but with the Church. The Church is the only group of people who can bring about the closing sign of the age—the preaching of this Gospel of the Kingdom. I am so glad Jesus said this. He did not suggest that some watered down, humanistic version of the Gospel would be sufficient, but stated that the same Gospel preached by Him and by the apostles must be the one preached in all the world as a witness to all the nations.

Revelation 7 tells us something about the people from these nations. John, describing what he saw in a vision, declares:

> After these things I looked, and behold, a great multitude which no one could number, of all nations, tribes, peoples, and tongues, standing before the throne and before the Lamb, clothed with white robes, with palm branches in their hands, and crying out with a loud voice, saying, "Salvation belongs to our God who sits on the throne, and to the Lamb!"
>
> Revelation 7:9–10

The great multitude of people, all of whom received salvation through faith in Jesus, the Lamb of God, comes from all nations, tribes, peoples and tongues. In other words, before the age can close, there has to be at least one representative in the Body of every nation, people, tribe and language on earth. I believe the reason is that God the Father is jealous for His Son's glory. Because Jesus was willing to suffer for all humankind, God will not allow the age to close until there is at least one representative from every tribe, people, nation and tongue who has received the salvation offered through Jesus, the Lamb of God.

This responsibility is ours, and it is a tremendous responsibility. When we consider all the tragedies—the suffering, sickness, hatred, wars and poverty—that mark the present age and that are increasing steadily, we have to face the fact that unless we do our job as quickly as we can, we are responsible for unnecessary, additional suffering. We must never forget our responsibility, and I say this with the utmost passion of my soul. As I said earlier, this is the verse that motivates me: "This gospel of the kingdom will be preached in all the world as a witness to all the nations, and then the end will come" (Matthew 24:14). I take the responsibility seriously.

We need to ask ourselves what we are living for. Is it for an easy life, the most we can get out of life, a better job, higher pay, a larger house, a faster car? Or are we living for this purpose—that this Gospel of the Kingdom may be proclaimed in all the world as a witness to all the nations?

When we stand before the judgment seat of Christ, as we must, one of the questions He is going to ask each of us individually is this: "What did you do to help the preaching of the Gospel of the Kingdom to all nations?" Will we have to stand before God one day and say, "I'm sorry, but I never really took this verse seriously. I just went on living my life as if the age were going to go on forever and all I had to do was look after number one and maybe number two." This is a desperately serious issue. I do not want to dwell on it, but it would be unfair if I did not point out the sobriety of this prophecy.

Each of us can do something. Each of us can contribute to this goal. In Matthew 9, Jesus says, "The harvest truly is plentiful, but the laborers are few." What did He say next? "Pray the Lord of the harvest" (Matthew 9:37–38). Everybody can pray; we are guilty if we do not pray. Most of us can give. If we view the whole world as it is today, with its population of more than 6.5 billion, most of us are wealthy. How can this be? We have beds to sleep on. Most of us have sheets on the beds. We can choose what we eat. And we have enough to eat. But there are millions and millions of people on earth who do not have those privileges. What are we doing with our money? Are we squandering it on self-indulgence while millions are starving? Not merely starving physically, but also starving spiritually for the Bread of Life?

To me, Matthew 24:14 is one of the most searching verses in the Bible: "This gospel of the kingdom will be preached in all the world as a witness to all the nations, and then the end will come." Jesus said that as a sign of the end the Gospel will be preached. If He said it will be preached, then it will be preached. The question becomes, What are we going to do about it?

6

The Chosen Are Gathered

Continuing with Jesus' teaching on signs of the end in Matthew 24, we come to a dramatic turn in His discourse. Up until now, the emphasis has been the whole world and all nations. In verse 15 the focus turns to a tiny little strip of territory at the east end of the Mediterranean, wrongly called *Palestine* by some, which means "the land of the Philistines." It is not the land of the Philistines; it is the land of Israel. Although we will focus on the topic of Israel and end time events in later chapters, I want to follow Jesus' presentation and the prophetic word He gives about Israel at this point.

By an everlasting covenant, God has given Israel forever to Abraham and his descendants, Isaac and Jacob, and their descendants. They are going to possess it. We cannot approach an end time study without considering our attitude toward that covenant and to the Jews themselves. There is no room for neutrality. We read in Exodus 3:

> God said to Moses, "Thus you shall say to the children of Israel: 'The LORD God of your fathers, the God of Abraham, the God of Isaac, and the God of Jacob, has sent me to you. This is My name forever, and this is My memorial to all generations.'"
>
> Exodus 3:15

Isn't that astonishing? Almighty God chose to be known forever as the God of three men. We need to give heed to that.

Let's remember another point made in Scripture. Jesus says quite clearly, "Salvation is from the Jews" (John 4:22, NASB). Whether or not we are Jewish, we must understand that we owe every spiritual blessing we have ever enjoyed to one people—the Jewish people. Without the Jews there would be no patriarchs, no prophets, no apostles, no Bible and no Savior.

I believe it is time we began to repay the debt. For the most part, unfortunately, the Church has done exactly the opposite. It has compounded the debt by centuries of prejudice, maligning and open persecution. Often when believers try to talk to Jewish people about Jesus, they find that a wall of reserve comes up. That is because, in the eyes of intelligent Jewish people who know history, the number one enemy of the Jewish people is the Christian Church. That may shock us, but it is true. And they can give many historical reasons why that is so.

This realization gives us new insight into Jesus' words in Matthew 24:28: "For wherever the carcass is, there the eagles [or vultures] will be gathered together." The first time I ever saw a vulture was in Egypt and it was rather dramatic. First, I saw a speck way up in the blue sky and it circled slowly and began to come lower and lower. Then other specks joined it, and as they circled they continued to come lower. I knew immediately that something was dying down on the ground, and they were just waiting for the creature's death to descend upon it. Jesus said, "When you see all the vultures circling around, you know where the carcass is."

This is simply a theory of mine, and I could be wrong, but I am inclined to think this verse refers to the way people are going to relate to the city of Jerusalem. All the vultures are already up in the air circling and coming lower because everybody wants a piece of the pie. The United States, Britain, the European Union, the Muslims, Russia—all like vultures over their prey.

God's Program for the Jews

Although we will see more and more the selfish intentions of peoples and nations toward Israel, we need to keep in mind that God has great plans for the Jews. First of all, let me point out that in Romans Paul says that "blindness in part has happened to Israel until the fullness [full number] of the Gentiles has come in. And so all Israel will be saved" (Romans 11:25–26). God has a program. At present, His program is to reap a vast harvest of Gentiles. But when that harvest is complete, all Israel will then be saved.

The fact is, many more Jews are now beginning to believe in Jesus as the Messiah. This is one of the signs we are coming to a period of transition from one age to the next—from the age of the Gentiles to the age when Israel will once again be the leading nation and the representative of God on earth among nations.

This brings us, then, to the warning Jesus gives in Matthew 24:15: "Therefore when you see the 'abomination of desolation,' spoken of by Daniel the prophet, standing in the holy place. . . ."

What is the "abomination of desolation"? There are endless theories about this, of course, but I believe it indicates the manifestation of the Antichrist. Twenty years ago I thought the appearance of the Antichrist was pretty remote. In fact, I almost laughed at people who were occupied with thoughts of it. Today, for me, the Antichrist seems very close at hand.

I have no question about what "the holy place" is: It is the Temple area in Jerusalem. At least two Scriptures relate directly to this. In the first one, the Lord is speaking to Solomon after he has finished building the Temple on a specific, designated site:

"I have heard your prayer and your supplication that you have made before Me; I have consecrated this house which you have built to put My name there forever, and My eyes and My heart will be there perpetually."

1 Kings 9:3

It does not matter who occupies that site. God has never withdrawn His promise. The second Scripture also confirms that God has sanctified this place: "For the LORD has chosen Zion [this area]; He has desired it for His dwelling place: 'This is My resting place forever; here I will dwell, for I have desired it'" (Psalm 132:13–14).

No matter how much men may desecrate it (and I am fully aware, as I mentioned earlier, that a Muslim temple stands there at this time) God has chosen that place, and, ultimately, it will be used for His purposes. It is the holy place.

Now, speaking about the Antichrist, Paul mentions him in connection with the coming of the Lord:

> Let no one deceive you by any means; for that Day will not come unless the falling away comes first, and the man of sin is revealed, the son of perdition [also known as the Antichrist, the man of lawlessness], who opposes and exalts himself above all that is called God or that is worshiped, so that he sits as God in the temple of God, showing himself that he is God.
>
> 2 Thessalonians 2:3–4

I believe that process is part of what is included in Matthew 24:15, and I believe it is very close at hand. I am not a person who speculates; it is an established fact that groups of Jewish people are preparing busily for the restoration of a Jewish temple.

It has also been discovered by Jewish archaeologists that the space the holy of holies occupied is not where the Dome of the Rock (Mosque of Omar) stands, but north of it. So it is conceivable that the Antichrist, who is going to be a master of politics, could strike a deal between the Jews and the Arabs by which the Arabs would retain the Mosque of Omar and the Jews would be permitted to build their temple just north, on the true site of the holy of holies. I am not saying it will happen that way, but it could.

We Must Act Quickly

When the Antichrist is manifested in that disputed area, Jesus says to act, and act quickly.

> "Then let those who are in Judea [what some people call the West Bank] flee to the mountains. Let him who is on the housetop not go down to take anything out of his house. And let him who is in the field not go back to get his clothes."
>
> Matthew 24:16–18

This use of *then* is dramatic. It speaks about a flight so rapid that there is no time to stop and take anything. In that part of the world many of the houses have flat roofs with side staircases on the outside of the house leading down to the ground. Jesus says that anyone who is on the roof when this happens should go down the staircase and not even enter the house. There is no time. The people should take off as fast as they can.

Then Jesus talks about a man in the field. He is in work clothes without a jacket. When this thing, whatever it is, happens, Jesus says to run, not even going back home to get clothes—for it is too late. We have noted that it will be such a hasty flight that pregnant women and women with nursing babies will be at a disadvantage.

As I pointed out in chapter 3, biblical prophecy sets parameters for prayer, and we cannot pray intelligently or effectively outside those parameters. Jesus has said that if we are living in Judea we are going to have to flee. We need not waste time praying that we will not have to flee. Instead, we should pray within the guidelines that we may not have to flee in the winter, for obvious reasons, or on the Sabbath. And as I pointed out, this last point assumes the establishment of the Jewish state because until that happens it will not make any difference whether we flee on the Sabbath or on some other day. That verse tells us a lot when we understand its implications.

The Great Tribulation

In Matthew 24:21, Jesus says, "For then." Notice: another *then*. "For then there will be great tribulation, such as has not been since the beginning of the world until this time, no, nor ever shall be."

Let's consider what has happened even in our days: the Holocaust with six million Jews cruelly murdered and burned in ovens; Stalin, who was responsible for the deaths of seven million people in the former Soviet Union; Mao Tse Tung, who acknowledged responsibility for the deaths of sixty million Chinese.

Yet Jesus is saying that something even worse than all of that is going to happen—something that has never happened until now and never will happen again. Scientists tell us there is enough nuclear explosive material in existence on earth to destroy the entire human race fifty times over. Such massive destruction is no longer a ridiculous impossibility.

An understanding of God's dealings with the Jews will give us a far clearer insight into all of Scripture than we could ever have without it. God's plan appears right in the middle of one of Paul's rather long sentences:

> . . . tribulation and anguish, on every soul of man who does evil, of the Jew first and also of the Greek [Gentile]; but glory,

honor, and peace to everyone who works what is good, to the Jew first and also to the Greek.

Romans 2:9–10

So there is an order in which God deals. When tribulation comes, it is to the Jew first and then to the Gentile. I tremble when I think about the Holocaust, because if that happened to six million Jews, what is going to happen to the Gentiles? It will never end with the Jews; they are the starting point. It is to the Jew *first*, and then to the Greek.

Jesus goes on to say: "Unless those days were shortened, no flesh [human being] would be saved; but for the elect's sake those days will be shortened" (Matthew 24:22).

The word *elect*, which occurs in this passage three times, is an important word meaning "chosen." It may be hard to accept, but Scripture indicates that God has those whom He has chosen. People like you and me. We are saved not because we chose Jesus, but because Jesus chose us. Jesus said to His disciples, "You did not choose Me, but I chose you" (John 15:16). Ephesians 1:4 tells us that God chose us in Christ before the foundation of the world.

When God chooses us, we have to make the decision to respond to His choice. But we never initiate His choice. God knows every one whom He has chosen. We are not "afterthoughts." We are not accidents looking for a place to happen. We are part of an eternal plan, one that includes a whole lot of people who are not yet believers. God knows each one of them, and He will not rest until He has gathered in every single one. That is why I am so deeply impressed by these words of Paul: "Therefore I endure all things for the sake of the elect, that they also may obtain the salvation which is in Christ Jesus with eternal glory" (2 Timothy 2:10). God has His chosen ones in every age, in every nation. Paul says that he is willing to go through whatever it takes to gather in the chosen ones.

Furthermore, the age will not close, Jesus tells us, until all the chosen ones have been gathered in: "Unless those days were shortened, no flesh would be saved; but for the elect's sake those days will be shortened." In other words, if God had not shortened the actual period of the Great Tribulation, no human being would remain alive.

We get further insight on the theme of the Great Tribulation from Revelation 7. In the last chapter we saw in this passage the reference to a throng—from all nations, tribes, peoples and tongues—that has gathered before the throne.

> Then one of the elders answered, saying to me, "Who are these arrayed in white robes, and where did they come from?" And I said to him, "Sir, you know." So he said to me, "These are the ones who come out of the great tribulation, and washed their robes and made them white in the blood of the Lamb."
>
> Revelation 7:13–14

John is not talking about those who *have* come out but who *are* coming out. John is actually seeing them streaming out of the Great Tribulation. By use of the word *the*, the English language indicates that there is only one tribulation. This is unique. It has never happened before and it will never happen again. Then the next verse gives these wonderful words: "Therefore they are before the throne of God, and serve Him day and night in His temple. And He who sits on the throne will dwell among them" (verse 15).

71

What a beautiful picture! It is something we need to focus on because we will have to go through a lot. We must not lose sight of the goal. Otherwise, we will get weary and, as the Bible says, "faint in [our] minds" (Hebrews 12:3, KJV). Let us never lose sight of God's planned close for the age. It is worth going through everything to end there.

7

Looking Up

Signs in the Heavens

At this point in His discourse, Jesus offers key signs that have a common theme: They have some relation to the skies. It is also at this point that He tells His disciples that He will return on the clouds and that the believers will meet Him in the air. These signs and promises turn our gaze heavenward.

The False Prophet

One very dramatic sign in the sky is accomplished by the false prophet who is the main supporter of the Antichrist. The magnitude of this person's abilities will apparently cause some to turn away from their faith. Our next *then* in Matthew 24 gives us this insight:

"Then if anyone says to you, 'Look, here is the Christ [Messiah]!' or 'There!' do not believe it. For false christs [messiahs] and false prophets will rise and show great signs and wonders to deceive, if possible, even the elect."

Matthew 24:23–24

Revelation 13 talks about the accomplishments of this false prophet:

He performs great signs, so that he even makes fire come down from heaven on the earth in the sight of men. And he deceives those who dwell on the earth by those signs which he was granted to do in the sight of the beast, telling those who dwell on the earth to make an image to the beast who was wounded by the sword and lived.

Revelation 13:13–14

This man will be able to make fire come down from heaven. I know of no preacher today who can do that—and yet he is a servant of Satan and uses these supernatural signs to deceive people.

Satan is capable of many dramatic signs and wonders. Many Christians have a tendency to think, *If it is supernatural, it must be from God.* That is not true, and we need to bear it in mind. In Acts 16 we read about a fortune-teller, a slave, who follows Paul and Silas in the streets saying, "These men are the servants of the Most High God, who proclaim to us the way of salvation" (Acts 16:17). She is the first person in Philippi to know who they are, but she is a servant of Satan. She has a satanic word of knowledge. How does Paul react? Does he make her a member of the church at Philippi? No, he casts the fortune-telling demon out of her!

I see so many Christians who are being set up for deception by satanic supernatural powers because of their fascination with the future through false signs and wonders. Truth is not established by signs; truth is established by the Word of God. Jesus said, "Your word is truth" (John 17:17). That is all we need to know. Anything contrary to the Word of God is not truth and is not from God.

Jesus says in Matthew 24:25, "See, I have told you beforehand." In other words, "You cannot say you have never been warned." In fact, those who read this book will never be able to say from now on that they have not been warned.

Falling Stars

There are more signs in the heavens that will announce His coming. In Matthew 24:29 we read: "Immediately after the tribulation of those days the sun will be darkened, and the moon will not give its light; the stars will fall from heaven, and the powers of the heavens will be shaken."

The words *the stars will fall from heaven* can be understood in various ways, but I do not think they refer to the stars we see at night. I am inclined to think they mean that the satanic angels in the heavenlies will be dethroned and cast down.

Let me give you two examples of this from the book of Revelation: "Then the third angel sounded: And a great star fell from heaven, burning like a torch, and it fell on a third of the rivers and on the springs of water. The name of the star is Wormwood" (Revelation 8:10–11). That is a satanic angel dislodged from heaven. And then at the beginning of chapter 9: "Then the fifth angel sounded: And I saw a star fallen from heaven to the earth. To him was given the key to the bottomless pit. And he opened the bottomless pit" (Revelation 9:1–2).

Satanic angels are depicted here as stars in the heaven. I do not envisage the whole body of the constellations falling. I envisage the powers of heaven—Satan's throne and his kingdom in the heavenlies—being disrupted to the point where his angels start to be shaken out of their positions.

Christ Comes in the Clouds

Some people espouse a theory that the Church is going to become so powerful politically, it will take over the world, set it neatly in order and offer it back to Jesus when He comes. This does not line up with what Scripture says. There is not the least indication that the world will be in good order when Jesus comes. On the contrary, it will be in the worst order ever. It will take Jesus, not the Church, to put it right.

> "Then the sign of the Son of Man will appear in heaven, and then all the tribes of the earth will mourn, and they will see the Son of Man coming on the clouds of heaven with power and great glory."
>
> Matthew 24:30

(Notice the two *then*s in this verse.)

Zechariah prophesies that all the tribes of Israel will mourn when they see their Messiah and recognize that they were the ones who crucified Him (see Zechariah 12:10–14). Apparently, this mourning will extend to all the tribes of the earth when they also see Jesus coming in glory.

Part of the reason people will be deceived by a false messiah is the belief that Jesus' return might be restricted to one locale. Jesus says something quite different: "Therefore if they say to you, 'Look, He is in the desert!' do not go out; or 'Look, He is in the inner rooms!' do not believe it. For as the lightning comes from the east and flashes to the west, so also will the coming of the Son of Man be" (Matthew 24:26–27).

Actually, I love to think of the Son of Man coming in the clouds of heaven with power and great glory. When He comes, there is going to be a triple glory, as indicated by the following verse: "For whoever is ashamed of Me and My words, of him the Son of Man will be ashamed when He comes in His own glory, and in His Father's, and of the holy angels" (Luke 9:26).

There will be Jesus' glory, the Father's glory and the glory of the angels. Isaiah 24:23 says that the sun and moon will be embarrassed because their light will be so dim and ineffective by comparison. This appeals to me. I can just imagine it. And furthermore, that light, though so brilliant, will not hurt our eyes. I am looking forward to that.

It is something worth waiting for, worth enduring for. If we lose sight of it we are going to get despondent, because things *are* going to get worse. Remember: The birth pangs are not going to diminish, they are going to increase.

The Raptured Church Rises

When the Lord comes back, descending from heaven, His appearance will be visible to the whole world, as will the rising up of His people to meet Him in the air—an event known as the Rapture. In the past I recall hearing a teaching that there would be a "secret rapture." My observation is that *secret* is the last word that should be used to describe the Rapture. Nothing more public will ever take place in human history, as we see by Jesus' description: "And He [the Lord] will send His angels with a great sound of a trumpet, and they will gather together His elect from the four winds, from one end of heaven to the other" (Matthew 24:31).

That is not secret! Note also that this is not talking about the Church being caught up; rather, it refers to those who remain on earth who are God's chosen ones.

First Thessalonians 4 gives a fuller description of what is going to happen at that point.

> But I do not want you to be ignorant, brethren, concerning those who have fallen asleep [Christians who have died], lest you sorrow as others who have no hope. For if we believe that Jesus died and rose again, even so God will bring with Him those who sleep in Jesus.
>
> For this we say to you by the word of the Lord, that we who are alive and remain until the coming of the Lord will by no means precede those who are asleep. For the Lord Himself will descend from heaven with a shout, with the voice of an archangel, and with the trumpet of God. And the dead in Christ will rise first. Then we who are alive and remain shall be caught up together with them in the clouds to meet the Lord in the air.
>
> 1 Thessalonians 4:13–17

There are two Greek words for air: one is *aither*, which gives us "ether"; the other is *aer*, which gives us "air." *Aer*, the word for the lower air contiguous with the earth's surface, is the word that is used here. In other words, Jesus is going to be pretty close to earth when we are caught up to meet Him.

How could anybody be unaware that something is going on when the Lord is shouting, the archangel is speaking and the trumpet of God is sounding?

Some people say the word *rapture* is not in the New Testament. That is quite true, but it depends on the translation used. The New Testament was not, of course, written originally in English. We could easily translate *we shall be caught up to meet the Lord in the air* in 1 Thessalonians 4:17 as "we shall be raptured to meet the Lord in the air." It would be a perfectly legitimate translation.

What about this word *rapture*? It is a fascinating, gripping word. The Greek word is *harpazo*. Several different passages in the New Testament use this word to give us a clear picture of what the Rapture is going to be like. First of all, three times in John 10 the word is used describing a wolf snatching a sheep from the fold. It is violent and sudden. (See John 10:12, 28–29.)

In Matthew 13:4, 19 it is used of a bird coming down, picking up a seed and carrying it off.

It is used several times in the New Testament of people caught up from the earth. After Philip had baptized the eunuch in Acts 8, for instance, he was caught away—he was raptured (see Acts 8:39). Paul speaks of a friend of his, mentioned twice in 2 Corinthians 12, who was caught up to the third heaven (see verses 2, 4). And Revelation 12:5 says, "A male Child . . . was caught up to God and His throne." (See also 1 Thessalonians 4:17.)

Four times in other passages the same word is used of taking somebody by force from a crowd or from some situation (see Matthew 11:12; John 6:15; Acts 23:10; Jude 23).

So here is a list of the features that the Rapture implies:

- It will happen without warning.
- It will be sudden and forceful.
- There will be no time to be getting ready. If we are in the process of getting ready, we will be too late.

Matthew 24, with another *then*, tells how quickly the Rapture will occur: "Then [at this time] two men will be in the field: one will be taken and the other left. Two women will be grinding at the mill: one will be taken and the other left" (Matthew 24:40–41).

The gospel of Luke says there will be two in one bed; one will be taken, the other left (see Luke 17:34). So here is a sudden, dramatic, eternal separation of people who are closest to one another: two women who work at the mill, the two men working in the field, even the two who share the same bed. When the Rapture comes, it will snatch one and leave the other. Which will we be? Snatched or left? It is important that we decide that issue.

> "Watch therefore, for you do not know what hour your Lord is coming. But know this, that if the master of the house had known what hour [or what watch of the night] the thief would come, he would have watched and not allowed his house to be broken into. Therefore you also be ready, for the Son of Man is coming at an hour you do not expect."
>
> Matthew 24:42–44

If the master had known what was going to happen, he would have stayed awake; he would have been watchful. So Jesus says, "Be ready." If we think we know, we really do not know. If we expect Him to come at a certain time, that will not be the time He is coming. I emphasize this because it has grieved me that millions of Christians have fallen for revelations that Jesus was coming on a certain day or a certain time. It is totally contrary to His teaching. We noted earlier these words from Mark 13:

> "Watch therefore, for you do not know when the master of the house is coming—in the evening, at midnight, at the crowing of the rooster, or in the morning—lest, coming suddenly, he find you sleeping. And what I say to you, I say to all: Watch!"
>
> Mark 13:35–37

We have to be watching. That does not mean we have to stay wide awake without sleep; it means we must be sensitive to what the Holy Spirit is saying so He can alert us at any time of the day or night.

The Fig Tree Puts on Leaves

There is one final sign Jesus gives in His discourse that involves looking up. It is the parable of the fig tree.

> "Now learn this parable from the fig tree: When its branch has already become tender and puts forth leaves, you know that summer is near. So you also, when you see all these things, know that it [or He] is near—at the doors! Assuredly,

I say to you, this generation will by no means pass away till all these things take place."

Matthew 24:32–34

Most people are familiar with the four seasons—spring, summer, autumn and winter—but not everyone. When I was teaching in East Africa, I had to explain to the students that in some parts of the world the trees lose their leaves. As you look up into their heights you see bare branches standing out against the sky. Then a change begins to happen. Tender little green buds begin to appear, bringing a greenish haze. When this happens, we know summer is coming.

In Luke's record of this discourse, Jesus says to look "at the fig tree, and all the trees" (Luke 21:29). In other words, change will happen with the fig tree first and then all the trees.

This is happening with the nations. For a long period they have just had bare branches, but now all around the world, the nations are putting on their leaves. In May 1948, Israel, the fig tree, put on its leaves. I was there when it happened. They got rid of the British, as other nations have also done, and said, "We're a people of our own. We have our own history, our own culture, our own language. We want to rule ourselves."

After that, other trees started putting on their leaves. In Africa alone at least fifty new nations have appeared. What is the motivation of these nations? Having lived among the Africans just two or three years before they became independent, sovereign nations, I can tell you their motivation. They said, "We are a people of our own. We have our own language. We may be able to speak English, but it's not our language.

We have our own customs; we have our own clothing. We want to be ourselves." What is that? It is an upsurge of nationalism, and it is happening all around the world. The trees are putting on their leaves.

Colonialism—control by one power over a dependent people—is a dirty word today, but that was not the case just fifty years ago. The new trend is *nationalism* or *ethnicity*. What is it? The trees putting on their leaves. Jesus says, in effect, when we see the trees putting on their leaves, we do not need to go to the public library to find out what is happening next. Summer is near. And when we see this happening in the world, we do not have to go to the church to ask the pastor. We can see for ourselves that a change is occurring.

This is one of the great signs of the close of the age—the rise of nationalism. It is almost universal and we have not seen the end of it yet. By this we know summer is near. We look up at the trees and see and know for ourselves.

We must stay awake. We must be alert. We must not be lulled into a carnal slumber. Many signs will occur in the heavens as the final days approach—dramatic, astonishing signs. By this we know that His coming is near.

8

Societies Like Ours
The Days of Noah and Lot

Through many different prophetic passages, the Bible presents a composite picture of what the world will look like as the present age draws to its close. It pulls together various significant events and trends that, in combination, will make the days immediately preceding the end of the present age a unique and distinctive period of human history.

Two of these prophetic passages describe actual historical societies, and Jesus tells us to take note of them. He says that in the day of His coming the world will be "just as it was" in the days of Noah and the days of Lot.

What were the distinctive features of these societies and how does our world compare? In this chapter we will view some of the main elements in the Bible's picture of the condition of the world in those days and make reference to scenes in the world around us today. The similarities are striking.

The Days of Noah

For the first element in the Bible's prophetic picture of these closing days, we continue with the words of Jesus in Matthew 24:

> "As the days of Noah were, so also will the coming of the Son of Man be. For as in the days before the flood, they were eating and drinking, marrying and giving in marriage, until the day that Noah entered the ark, and did not know until the flood came and took them all away, so also will the coming of the Son of Man be."
>
> Matthew 24:37–39

The parallel account in Luke 17:26 gives this wording: "As it was in the days of Noah, so it will be also in the days of the Son of Man [the days prior to the return of Jesus]." To understand the days prior to Jesus' return, therefore, we need to find out what the days of Noah were like. For a description of those days, we will look in the book of Genesis for the main elements.

> Now it came to pass, when men began to multiply on the face of the earth, and daughters were born to them, that the sons of God saw the daughters of men, that they were beautiful; and they took wives for themselves of all whom they chose. And the LORD said, "My Spirit shall not strive with man forever, for he is indeed flesh; yet his days shall be one

hundred and twenty years." There were giants [Nephilim, NASB] on the earth in those days, and also afterward, when the sons of God came in to the daughters of men and they bore children to them. Those were the mighty men who were of old, men of renown.

Genesis 6:1–4

Personally, I believe the words *the sons of God*, used here and elsewhere, are a designation for angels. The picture is one of angelic beings from a supernatural plane, a plane above the level of the earth, who came down and had sexual relationships with the daughters of men, or human women. We also see that when this began to happen, God set a definite time limit to the period for which He would tolerate this kind of unnatural relationship: one hundred and twenty years.

The word *Nephilim* is a Hebrew word directly related to the Hebrew verb for *to fall*, which is *naphal*. So *Nephilim* means "the fallen ones." It is clear to me that it means fallen angels. In the *New American Standard Bible*, this verse reads:

The Nephilim [fallen angels] were on the earth in those days, and also afterward, when the sons of God [the angels] came in to the daughters of men, and they bore children to them. Those were the mighty men who were of old, men of renown.

Genesis 6:4, NASB

Some people find this picture of unnatural relationship between fallen angels from the heavenly realm and human women somewhat surprising, astonishing or hard to receive.

Educated as I was in the classics in Britain in Latin and Greek, I have no difficulty in believing it. The history and the mythology of both the Romans and the Greeks are filled with stories of people whom they called "gods" (whom we would call "fallen angels") having sexual relationships with human women.

That is the initial picture of the specific conditions of the age of Noah. We could perhaps sum it up with a phrase like this: *In the time of Noah there was intense pressure and penetration of the human race from the occult realm, an unseen spiritual realm.*

The next verse in Genesis 6 gives us more description of the world in Noah's day: "Then the LORD saw that the wickedness of man was great in the earth, and that every intent of the thoughts of his heart was only evil continually" (Genesis 6:5).

Here the emphasis is on man's inner experience, what is going on inside his mind and heart. Scripture says that his imagination—his thoughts and his intentions—was all evil. We could sum it up, perhaps, with the phrase *universal corruption of thought-life.* Everything had been contaminated: images, speech and concepts—all permeated by something impure and unclean.

The next distinctive feature of the age of Noah was that "the earth was filled with violence" (Genesis 6:11). There was apparently a sudden upsurge of crimes of violence. Men became so violent in their acts and attitudes that violence as a feature of life was accepted as commonplace.

If there is one feature of Noah's day being repeated in our day, it is pervasive violence. I am old enough to remember when ladies could walk safely in the streets of the main cities of both Britain and the United States—without fear, even at night. Now it is not safe to walk even in the day-time in some of our major cities. We have come to accept this as a fact, but it is a fact that is comparatively recent. We are inured to this; it is a part of life. The earth is filled with violence.

In the next verse we have another aspect of the days of Noah: "So God looked upon the earth, and indeed it was corrupt; for all flesh had corrupted their way on the earth" (Genesis 6:12).

That one word, *corrupt*, probably sums up the condition as well as any one word could. There was total corruption of all the relationships we associate with the flesh. Primarily and particularly, the sex life and relationships of the time had become corrupted and unnatural, resulting in sexual degradation and perversion.

Today this is commonplace. About thirty years ago, I came to realize that sexual perversion was being practiced by churchgoing Christians—especially the abuse of young boys and girls. But nobody talked about it in those days, and it was a shock to me when I discovered that it was happening. Today everybody knows it is happening in the churches. Among the unsaved, sexual perversion is fashionable—there are many unconverted people who boast of it. There are programs on television that actually take delight in exposing all the nasty details.

If we put these pictures together, we can single out four distinctive aspects of the days of Noah. As I go through this list again, let's consider how far the same is true of our society and our culture all around us today.

1. This was a culture with intense pressure and penetration from the occult realm. There were unnatural relationships between beings of different orders—spirit beings from a higher realm and human beings on earth.
2. It had universal corruption of thought.
3. It had rampant violence, with crimes of violence increasing dramatically.
4. It had widespread sexual corruption and perversion.

How does that match up with our society and our culture today? Do we see an increasing penetration of normal human life by occult forces and influences? Do we find men's thoughts being corrupted, language degenerating and society filled with impure and unclean images and suggestions? Is the earth filled with violence? Do we see sexual corruption and perversion around us in ever-increasing measure? Obviously, the answer to those questions is yes.

The Days of Lot

Not only does Jesus compare this closing period with the days of Noah, but also with the days of Lot:

> "As it was in the days of Noah, so it will be also in the days of the Son of man. . . . Likewise as it was also in the days of Lot: They ate, they drank, they bought, they sold, they planted, they built; but on the day that Lot went out of Sodom it rained fire and brimstone from heaven and destroyed them all. Even so will it be in the day when the Son of Man is revealed."
>
> Luke 17:26, 28–30

We have to look primarily in Genesis 19 to get an accurate and gripping picture of what Jesus was talking about.

The two angels arrived at Sodom [where Lot lived] in the evening, and Lot was sitting in the gateway of the city. When he saw them, he got up to meet them and bowed down with his face to the ground. "My lords," he said, "please turn aside to your servant's house. You can wash your feet and spend the night and then go on your way early in the morning."

"No," they answered, "we will spend the night in the square."

But he insisted so strongly that they did go with him and entered his house. He prepared a meal for them, baking bread without yeast, and they ate. Before they had gone to bed, all the men from every part of the city of Sodom—both young and old—surrounded the house. They called to Lot, "Where are the men who came to you tonight? Bring them out to us so that we can have sex with them."

Lot went outside to meet them and shut the door behind him and said, "No, my friends. Don't do this wicked thing. Look, I have two daughters who have never slept with a man. Let me bring them out to you, and you can do what you like with them. But don't do anything to these men, for they have come under the protection of my roof."

"Get out of our way," they replied. And they said, "This fellow came here as an alien, and now he wants to play the judge! We'll treat you worse than them." They kept bringing pressure on Lot and moved forward to break down the door.

But the men inside [the angels] reached out and pulled Lot back into the house and shut the door. Then they struck the men who were at the door of the house, young and old, with blindness so that they could not find the door.

The two men said to Lot, "Do you have anyone else here—
sons-in-law, sons or daughters, or anyone else in the city
who belongs to you? Get them out of here, because we are
going to destroy this place. The outcry to the Lord against
its people is so great that he has sent us to destroy it."

Genesis 19:1–13, niv

The name of that city, Sodom, in the English language,
was applied to a particular form of sexual perversion called
"sodomy," now misnamed as "being gay." Probably the most
common word used today is *homosexuality*. In many ways,
the time of Lot was similar to the time of Noah. There was,
however, in Lot's time a special emphasis on homosexuality—
men desiring sexual relationships with other men.

This particular version of homosexuality was brazen; it
came right out in the open. It made no pretense and offered
no concealment. It was not passive; it was aggressive. It went
out looking for its victims, searched for them with determina-
tion and was prepared to resort to physical violence.

In addition, it embraced both young and old. Genesis 19
describes "all the men from the city—both young and old."
This city's male population was apparently totally given over
to this brazen, aggressive, violent form of homosexuality.

And, finally, it ignored accepted standards of behavior.
In those days, for a man to be asked to bring his guests out
and submit them to shame and degradation was the most
terrible request that could be made.

We single out four distinctive aspects from this society
as well:

1. This was a culture or civilization given over to this
   unnatural sexual relationship primarily among the

men. (We read nothing in particular about the women there.)

2. Its perversion was brazen, aggressive and violent.

3. It embraced both the young and the old.

4. It ignored all accepted standards of behavior.

We can consider what we see in the United States and in the so-called Western world today, and draw our own conclusions. From my own observation in the past several decades, this particular trend has increased with unbelievable rapidity.

Some of God's judgments are what we call "exemplary" (serving as a model), like the judgments on Sodom, Lot's city, and on Gomorrah. The people of Sodom and Gomorrah were destroyed, but that is not the way God judges everybody who is guilty of those practices. It is an exemplary judgment to show, once and for all, what God really thinks about this behavior. We see a similar model in the judgment on Ananias and Sapphira, who were hypocrites, claiming to give more to the work of God than they actually did, and they perished (see Acts 5:1–11). In that case, if God judged all who were hypocritical about what they give to Him, our churches would have far fewer members! But God does not do that. He declared, once and for all, what He thinks about hypocrisy—and about the behavior of the citizens of Sodom and Gomorrah.

The Real Sin of Sodom

I want to add one important note. Many people think the real sin of Sodom was homosexuality, but that is not what God charges it with. This amazed me when I first discovered it. Ezekiel 16, addressed to the city of Jerusalem, compares Jerusalem with Sodom, and this is what the Lord says about Sodom:

> "Look, this was the iniquity of your sister Sodom: She and her daughter [that is, her fellow cities] had pride, fullness of food, and abundance of idleness; neither did she strengthen the hand of the poor and needy."
>
> Ezekiel 16:49

There is no mention of homosexuality. I am not saying that God is indifferent toward homosexuality. Far from it. But the basic sins of Sodom were selfishness, carnality, self-indulgence, looking after number one. This is just my opinion, but I believe the Sodom kind of culture will always produce homosexuality. That is why we have so many homosexuals in the world today—because the sins of our day are just like the sins of Sodom: "Pride, fullness of food, and abundance of idleness; neither did she strengthen the hand of the poor and needy."

How well does that describe our contemporary culture? Thankfully, there are wonderful exceptions to this. But they are exceptions. We can lament the upsurge of homosexuality, but I believe the Sodom type of culture as described in Ezekiel 16 will always produce homosexuality. Homosexuality is not the root. The root is selfishness, self-indulgence and indifference to others.

One Final Factor

There is one final aspect of the last days that Jesus points to, and it was present in the societies of both Noah and Lot.

Jesus speaks about these activities: "They ate, they drank, they married wives, they were given in marriage. . . . Likewise as it was also in the days of Lot: They ate, they drank, they bought, they sold, they planted, they built" (Luke 17:27–28).

Jesus mentions eight specific activities: eating, drinking, marrying, giving in marriage, buying, selling, building and planting. There is nothing intrinsically sinful about any of those activities. So what was the problem? The problem was they were so immersed in those activities they did not recognize the days in which they were living. I would sum that problem up in one word: *materialism.* They were so immersed in the material they no longer had any understanding or alertness for the spiritual and the eternal.

The final feature of the days of Noah and Lot, then, was *materialism.* How much materialism is there in the world today? I would say Western civilization is virtually inundated with it, and it is by no means excluded from the Church. There are many professing Christians who, in their hearts, are just as materialistic as unbelievers. Maybe they are a little less demonstrative about it. Maybe it is not as apparent in their lifestyles. But they are absorbed with materialism. Jesus warned us that if we are sucked into the pit of materialism, we will not be ready when He comes. We will be in the same category as the people of Noah's and Lot's days.

The Positive Side: Warning for Survival

I have been presenting the evil elements conspicuous in the days of both Noah and Lot. As we have seen, various forms of evil were rampant. It would be wrong, however, for me to close this picture of the days of Noah and of Lot without also presenting the positive side of the picture, for there was a positive side in two main respects.

There is a good side to the days of Noah, for Genesis 6:9 says, "Noah walked with God." There was one man out of all those people who had an intimate, personal relationship with God. God could speak to him and tell him how He viewed the situation and the judgment He was going to bring. For us as believers, Noah sets a pattern to follow. Noah and his family were the only survivors. It seems clear to me that only those people who live like Noah and his family will survive today. Hebrews 11 has just one verse about Noah:

By faith Noah, being divinely warned of things not yet seen, moved with godly fear, prepared an ark for the saving of his household, by which he condemned the world and became heir of the righteousness which is according to faith.

Hebrews 11:7

Here is the feature I want to point out: Noah was not left in ignorance of what was coming. As God's faithful servant, he received—directly from God—supernatural revelation of what was to happen on the earth and how he and his family could prepare for it, face it and survive. God warned Noah in advance and showed him a way through.

Just as the negative elements of the story apply to the present time, so should this positive element. Tremendous dangers face us—catastrophes and judgments we cannot fully measure or ascertain. But, in the midst of it all, I believe God will still warn His faithful servants and show them a way of survival.

Jesus promised this to His disciples in the Person of the Holy Spirit:

> "However, when He, the Spirit of truth, has come, He will guide you into all truth; for He will not speak on His own authority, but whatever He hears He will speak; and He will tell you things to come."

John 16:13

It is very important that we see this ministry of the Holy Spirit to God's believing people. He will tell us what is yet to come—not necessarily *all* that is to come, but all we need to know for survival and for fulfilling God's purpose. The Holy Spirit will reveal this to us supernaturally just as He did to Noah.

In the case of Lot, God sent angels to protect and deliver him. In these days of crisis and pressure, we can expect God in His faithfulness to do the same where it is necessary for us. I believe we are entitled to expect the supernatural presence and assistance of angels. The writer of Hebrews says ministering spirits are sent forth to minister to the heirs of salvation—the believers of this time (see Hebrews 1:14).

Although there is much that is evil and frightening in the picture of the days of Noah and Lot—and much also that agrees with the evil and frightening aspects of our time—we must also look at the positive side. We need to see that there is never a situation for which God does not have an answer prepared in advance. God will give His servants supernatural warning of what is to come and show us how to survive. He also sends angels to help, to protect and to deliver. We can expect these good things from God in our day.

9

The Impact
of Christ's Return

We have been working our way systematically through the events that will coincide with the end of the age as explained in Matthew 24. We have reached a decisive point in the discourse of Jesus, as we have constructed the "spine" of His teaching. Now we can look at the impact of Christ's return on four different categories of people who are symbolic of those who will witness His return: the faithful and wise servant, the ten virgins, the servants given talents, and the sheep and goat nations.

The Faithful and Wise Servant

The first category, contained in Matthew 24:45–51, speaks about those whom the Lord has set in His household to care for the needs of His people—specifically, to give them the appropriate food at the right time.

> "Who then is a faithful and wise servant, whom his master made ruler over his household, to give them food in due season? Blessed is that servant whom his master, when he comes, will find so doing. Assuredly, I say to you that he will make him ruler over all his goods. But if that evil servant says in his heart, 'My master is delaying his coming,' and begins to beat his fellow servants, and to eat and drink with the drunkards, the master of that servant will come on a day when he is not looking for him and at an hour that he is not aware of, and will cut him in two and appoint him his portion with the hypocrites. There shall be weeping and gnashing of teeth."

What kind of person does this *servant/ruler* indicate for us today? The description is found in 1 Peter:

> The elders who are among you I exhort, I who am a fellow elder and a witness of the sufferings of Christ, and also a partaker of the glory that will be revealed: Shepherd the flock of God which is among you, serving as overseers, not by compulsion but willingly, not for dishonest gain but eagerly; nor as being lords over those entrusted to you, but being examples to the flock; and when the Chief Shepherd appears, you will receive the crown of glory that does not fade away.
>
> 1 Peter 5:1–4

This speaks about those whom the Lord has placed in His flock as overseers. The overseers—the pastors, the shepherds, the elders, the apostles (for Peter was an apostle)—are appointed by Jesus *in* the flock and *over* the flock. Let's not emphasize one preposition at the expense of the other. They are not just *over* the flock; they are also *in* the flock. This is true of all the fivefold ministries mentioned in Ephesians 4:11.

When Peter says, in verse 2 above, "Shepherd the flock of God which is among you," he is not talking to a superior class of people who live on a different level from the rest of God's people. He is talking about those who live among God's people, but yet have a special responsibility over them. Peter's warning is to his fellow elders—because when an apostle becomes resident in the city, he has the position of an elder. Elders must be careful how they handle their responsibilities because one day they will have to give an account.

Here is the picture Jesus draws: "Who then is a faithful and wise servant, whom his master made ruler over his household [or whom his master has appointed within his household], to give them food in due season?" (Matthew 24:45).

The first requirement for such a servant/ruler is not success, but faithfulness. I was a missionary in two areas at different times, and in each place I recognized that missionaries before me had labored faithfully, had even laid down their lives, yet had seen very little obvious fruit. I had to remind myself, *God forbid that I should ever think that I am more successful than they are, because if they had not been here first, the way would not have been prepared for me.* God does not look for success as the world understands it. He looks for faithfulness. "Who is that faithful servant?" Success is accomplishing faithfully the task allotted to you by the Lord.

We see that the task here is to give God's people their food in due season. That is a pastoral task, a shepherd's task. A true pastor knows exactly what his particular flock needs. It may be quite different from what another flock needs at the same time. When I go to minister to a congregation, I always like to inquire of the pastor or the pastoral staff: What do you think your people need particularly? It requires sensitivity.

And then Jesus tells us the reward of that kind of service: "Blessed is that servant whom his master, when he comes, will find so doing. Assuredly, I say to you that he will make him ruler over all his goods" (Matthew 24:46–47).

The Other Side of the Picture

Faithfulness in this life leads to promotion in the next life. This is a solemn thought. The way we conduct ourselves in this world will determine what we will be for eternity. There is no substitute for faithfulness.

Now we come to the *but*—the other side of the picture: "But if that evil servant says in his heart, 'My master is delaying his coming,' and begins to beat his fellow servants, and to eat and drink with the drunkards" (Matthew 24:48–49).

If we look at the picture of the judgment seat of Christ described in Romans 14 and 2 Corinthians 5 from which He will judge the Church, we find there are only two categories: good or evil. There is nothing in between. We in the Church have invented a third category: not good, but not evil either. In God's view, that category does not exist. If you are not good, you are evil.

A lot of people in our churches today are "fence sitters." They are not really committed, but they do not want to be classed as unbelievers. When the Holy Spirit comes to the Church, however, one of the first things He does is to electrify the fence! That is why some people do not welcome the Holy Spirit—they want to stay comfortably seated on the fence.

What is the feature of this evil servant? He says, "My master is delaying his coming." In other words, he has lost the vision of the imminent reality of the Lord's return. In churches where the coming of the Lord Jesus is not proclaimed as a reality, the standards of holiness will never be like those of the New Testament. Jesus' return is an essential truth to produce holiness in God's people.

The evil servant says, "My master has been away a long time; I haven't heard anything about him. I haven't really been in close touch with him. I can live it up." He becomes domineering and begins to beat his fellow servants. It is easy for people who occupy the position of pastors to become domineering and controlling. Yet God will never put His anointing on something that we humans seek to control. God says, *Unless I'm allowed to be in charge, you can go through your religious procedures, you can use all the words and the titles. But the result will not be what comes only from the anointing of the Holy Spirit.*

The unfaithful pastor or leader in Matthew 24 also becomes involved in drinking. And not merely drinking, but drinking with the wrong company—drinking with the drunkards.

Please understand, I am not preaching against drinking, because someone can be just as wrong on the other side with all his legalism. I have been a Pentecostal long enough to know what legalism is! The pathway that leads to life is a straight and narrow way, and there are ditches on either side. One side is self-indulgence or carnality. You can fall into that ditch. Then you struggle out of that ditch and if you are not careful you can fall into the opposite ditch, which is legalism. We have to walk between the two.

Let's look again at Jesus' words about this evil servant:

"The master of that servant will come on a day when he is not looking for him and at an hour that he is not aware of, and will cut him in two and appoint him his portion with the hypocrites. There shall be weeping and gnashing of teeth."

Matthew 24:50–51

When the master comes, the servant is not ready for him. As a result, the master will come and cut him in two. The master, of course, is Jesus. Do we realize that Jesus is capable of cutting somebody in two? We need to bear in mind that not only is He the Savior, He is also the judge. He is just as thorough and faithful in judging us as He is in saving us. If we do not live for Him as Savior, we will encounter Him as Judge. Those are the only two options before any of us.

Weeping and Gnashing of Teeth

Then He says, "There shall be weeping and gnashing of teeth." Jesus uses that phrase about five times in the New Testament for a certain category of people: those who have known all about Him, who have heard all the truth, who have been close to it perhaps all their lives, but never really committed themselves. And there will be weeping and gnashing of teeth because they will suddenly realize they were so close all their lives, they could have stepped in at any moment. But they never did, and now they are shut out forever.

Jesus' first use of this phrase, found in Matthew 8:12, refers to "the sons of the kingdom." Jesus is speaking to His fellow Jews and saying, "You are rejecting Me, but the Gentiles will come. They will enter the Kingdom, and you will be shut out. And there will be weeping and gnashing of teeth." These are people who have known it all, who had every opportunity but never availed themselves.

In Matthew 13:42 this phrase is used of the people who are the tares in the wheat field, looking exactly like the wheat but never producing fruit. Jesus says the angels will come and root them up and "cast them into the furnace of fire. There will be wailing and gnashing of teeth." All their lives these people have been close to it, right in the middle of it, but they never entered into it.

In Matthew 22:12–13, in the parable of the wedding feast, there is one guest who comes in without a wedding garment. Actually, he did not even have to buy his wedding garment—the host provided it. So it is sheer audacity and presumption to walk in without one. When the master of the feast sees him, he says, "How did you come in here without a wedding garment?" The man is speechless. The master says, "Bind him hand and foot, take him away, and cast him into outer darkness; there will be weeping and gnashing of teeth." Again, we see that this is somebody who knew all about it. He had received an invitation to the feast but he did not bother to put on the appropriate garment, which is the righteousness of Jesus Christ.

In Matthew 25:30, we find the "one talent" servant, and again it involves weeping and gnashing of teeth. (We will be looking at this story in a moment.)

Finally, in Luke 13:26–28, there are people who say to Jesus, "We ate and drank in Your presence, and You taught in our streets." And Jesus says to them, "I do not know you. . . . Depart from Me, all you workers of iniquity." And outside there will be weeping and gnashing of teeth.

The Ten Virgins

Now we come to the next category of people who will feel the impact of the coming of the Lord, found at the beginning of Matthew 25. And here we find another *then*.

In the Bible, ten is the representative number of a congregation. In Judaism, a *minion*—at least ten persons—must be present before public prayers can be offered. My thought here is that these virgins basically represent churchgoers.

"Then the kingdom of heaven shall be likened to ten virgins who took their lamps and went out to meet the bridegroom. Now five of them were wise, and five were foolish. Those who were foolish took their lamps and took no oil with them, but the wise took oil in their vessels with their lamps. But while the bridegroom was delayed, they all slumbered and slept.

"And at midnight a cry was heard: 'Behold, the bridegroom is coming; go out to meet him!' Then all those virgins arose and trimmed their lamps. And the foolish said to the wise, 'Give us some of your oil, for our lamps are going out.' But the wise answered, saying, 'No, lest there should not be enough for us and you; but go rather to those who sell, and buy for yourselves.' And while they went to buy, the bridegroom came, and those who were ready went in with him to the wedding; and the door was shut.

"Afterward the other virgins came also, saying, 'Lord, Lord, open to us!' But he answered and said, 'Assuredly, I say to you, I do not know you.'

"Watch therefore, for you know neither the day nor the hour in which the Son of Man is coming."

Matthew 25:1–13

Here are three points about those ten virgins that are common to them all:

- They all expect the bridegroom. They all know the bridegroom is coming. They are not unbelievers.
- They all have lamps and oil. Almost always, oil is a type of the Holy Spirit. They all have the Holy Spirit in their lives.
- All of them slumber, both the wise and the foolish.

There is only one difference: *the amount of oil they have.* The wise have oil enough and some to spare. The foolish do not have a reserve of oil. We need to note again that there is no middle category—either we are wise or we are foolish.

Let's look at what Paul says in Ephesians, and apply it to the need for a sufficient amount of oil: "Do not be drunk with wine, in which is dissipation; but be filled with the [Holy] Spirit" (Ephesians 5:18).

Most of us would agree that the negative command applies: "Do not be drunk with wine." That is a sin. But why is it that so many religious people focus on the negative and do not attend to the positive? That same command says, "Be filled with the Holy Spirit." If it is a sin to be drunk with wine, it is also a sin not to be filled with the Holy Spirit.

And that means "be continually filled and refilled." It is not just a one-time infilling.

I know what some will say: "I was baptized in the Holy Spirit ten years ago and I spoke in tongues." That is wonderful! But that was ten years ago. What has happened in the meanwhile? People who make it a once-for-all experience tend to be the least sensitive to the leading of the Holy Spirit. They have it all wrapped up in the packet they received when they spoke in tongues. But that is not sufficient.

Paul says to the Corinthians, "I speak with tongues more than you all" (1 Corinthians 14:18). Obviously they do a lot of speaking in tongues, but Paul does more. We have to be filled and refilled with the Holy Spirit continually. All of these ten virgins have the initial filling, but because they do not all have the continual refilling, some are not ready.

It is interesting to note that the wise virgins say to the foolish: "Go and buy oil." It has to be bought; it is not a gift. Initially, the Holy Spirit is a gift. But if we want to remain filled with the Holy Spirit, there is a price to pay. What Jesus says to the church of Laodicea is in so many ways a picture of churches in countries like America today:

> "Because you say, 'I am rich, have become wealthy, and have need of nothing'—and do not know that you are wretched, miserable, poor, blind, and naked—I counsel you to buy from Me gold refined in the fire, that you may be rich; and white garments, that you may be clothed, that the shame of your nakedness may not be revealed."
>
> Revelation 3:17–18

Does Jesus approve of people being rich, wealthy and in need of nothing? Not the least bit. I marvel that people can be in that condition and never even know it!

But Jesus gives us some advice. "I'm not going to give the gold to you; you have to buy it from Me." In the ancient world, gold was valueless unless it had been tested by fire. Gold represents here faith that has stood the test of fire. Jesus says, "You'll have to pay for it by endurance. You'll have to hold out under the test." Not everything in the Christian life is free. There are things we have to pay for.

Note also Jesus' evaluation of two churches in the book of Revelation in comparison with contemporary Christianity. One church, the church of Smyrna, is poor and persecuted and does not have much. But Jesus says, "You are rich" (Revelation 2:9). The church of Laodicea has it all, but He says, "You are poor." What would He say to many churches today? Would He say, "You are rich," or "You are poor"? Man's evaluation is often the opposite of God's. According to Jesus, that which is "highly esteemed among men is an abomination in the sight of God" (Luke 16:15).

The foolish virgins who have to go buy oil find that it is too late. When they return, the door is shut, and Jesus says, "I never knew you." I understand that to mean they were never among God's elect. They had come in, but God knew they would never pass the test.

How do we buy oil? By prayer, by Bible reading, by waiting on God. It takes time and it takes effort. It does not just happen. We have to make the decision. Have we bought our oil?

The Servants Given Talents

The next group feeling the impact of the Lord's return is the servants with the talents. The passage is lengthy, but it is important for us:

"For the kingdom of heaven is like a man traveling to a far country, who called his own servants and delivered his goods to them. And to one he gave five talents, to another two, and to another one, to each according to his own ability; and immediately he went on a journey. Then he who had received the five talents went and traded with them, and made another five talents. And likewise he who had received two gained two more also. But he who had received one went and dug in the ground, and hid his lord's money. After a long time the lord of those servants came and settled accounts with them.

"So he who had received five talents came and brought five other talents, saying, 'Lord, you delivered to me five talents; look, I have gained five more talents besides them.' His lord said to him, 'Well done, good and faithful servant; you were faithful over a few things, I will make you ruler over many things. Enter into the joy of your lord.' He also who had received two talents came and said, 'Lord, you delivered to me two talents; look, I have gained two more talents besides them.' His lord said to him, 'Well done, good and faithful servant; you have been faithful over a few things, I will make you ruler over many things. Enter into the joy of your lord.'

"Then he who had received the one talent came and said, 'Lord, I knew you to be a hard man, reaping where you have not sown, and gathering where you have not scattered seed. And I was afraid, and went and hid your talent in the ground. Look, there you have what is yours.'

108

"But his lord answered and said to him, 'You wicked and lazy servant, you knew that I reap where I have not sown, and gather where I have not scattered seed. So you ought to have deposited my money with the bankers, and at my coming I would have received back my own with interest. So take the talent from him, and give it to him who has ten talents.

"'For to everyone who has, more will be given, and he will have abundance; but from him who does not have, even what he has will be taken away. And cast the unprofitable servant into the outer darkness. There will be weeping and gnashing of teeth.'"

Matthew 25:14–30

The servants who make a profit each gain 100 percent. The one with five gains five, the one with two gains two, and the words of commendation are exactly alike: "Well done, good and faithful servant. Enter into the joy of your lord." The Lord does not commend the five-talent servant more than the two-talent servant. This tells me that what He is looking for is increase. Because the increase is proportionate in both (100 percent), he gives them exactly the same commendation.

As we noted previously regarding His overseers, God is looking for faithfulness rather than success. And each of these servants with talents is rewarded with corresponding authority in Christ's Kingdom. In other words, the way we serve in this life will determine our position in the Kingdom of God throughout eternity.

The Effects of Fear

What about the third unfaithful servant? First, he acts out of fear, which is not the right motive for serving the Lord.

Love should be our motive. Jesus says to us, "If anyone loves Me, he will keep My word" (John 14:23). As Paul explains, "The love of Christ compels [or constrains] us" (2 Corinthians 5:14)—that is the only fruitful motivation for service.

The next lesson is equally important for all Christians. Laziness is wickedness: "You wicked and lazy servant." Many have a religious set of values that are not always realistic. Most churches will not tolerate drunkenness, and quite rightly. But many churches will tolerate laziness, and actually, God's condemnation of laziness is more severe than His condemnation of drunkenness. We have people in our churches who really do very little for God. They are too lazy to read the Bible, too lazy to get up and pray, too lazy to go out to a street meeting. They just sit in the pews, are nice to everybody, do nobody any harm and put some money in the collection plate. We do not think about them as wicked, but Jesus does. He says laziness is wickedness.

Then the master in the story says, "You should have deposited the money with the bankers and you would have received interest." That, to me, is convincing evidence that it is not always sinful to receive interest. The laws against usury in the Old Testament applied to someone who made a loan to a fellow Jew. It would be wicked, if he was in need, to require interest on that loan. But if we lend to somebody who is in a business that is going to make a profit, we are entitled to a legitimate share of his profit. That is the way I understand it. Jesus certainly expects this servant to open a savings account if he cannot do anything else.

What does this mean for us? I suggest that to "put the money in the bank" means saying to ourselves, "I don't have a really strong ministry of my own, but I do have one talent to invest. I'll invest it in the ministry of another—someone who has a ministry bringing forth fruit in the Kingdom. I'll give him my contribution. I'll invest there by putting myself at his disposal. If necessary, I'll lick envelopes." Then when the Lord comes, He will get His own with interest. We should not just sit idly and say, "I have only one talent, so there's not much I can do."

Psychologically, it is the one-talent person who fails. The man who has five talents is excited about the prospect. He knows he will do something. The man who has two talents is excited. But the man who has one talent convinces himself that there is not much he can accomplish. It is a terribly dangerous attitude.

Use It or Lose It

Here is the next truth: Not to use is to lose. God gives spiritual gifts unconditionally; He never demands them back. But if we do not use them, we will lose them.

God gave me a gift in the early 1970s—some of you are familiar with it. It is faith for people whose legs are unequal. Through prayer, I have seen probably thousands of unequal legs made equal. Some of my good friends have said to me, "Dear friend, listen. You've got a good reputation as a scholarly Bible teacher. Don't spoil it by going around and kneeling in front of people and lengthening their legs." So I thought, *Maybe that's good advice. I'll pray about it.*

When I prayed I felt the Lord say to me, *I have given you a gift. There are two things you can do. You can use it and get more, or you can choose not to use it and lose it.* I said, "Lord, I'll choose the first." Each one of us has a gift of some

111

sort. If we do not use it, we will lose it. If we use it, we will get more. The choice is ours.

We need to note that the rejection of this unfaithful servant was final. He was cast into outer darkness. Where he went, there was weeping and gnashing of teeth.

The Parable of the Minas

A parallel parable, Luke 19, is the parable of the minas. In the old King James Version it is called the parable of the pounds. Here are some differences between the parable of the talents in Matthew 24 and the parable of the minas in Luke 19. In Luke, each of the ten servants receives one mina, whereas in Matthew each servant receives according to his ability. Jesus knows how much He can trust each one with.

At the end of the parable in Luke, one has gained ten minas; he makes a tenfold increase. His master says to him, "Well done, good servant; because you were faithful in a very little, have authority over ten cities" (verse 17). Another one has gained five minas and his master says to him, "You also be over five cities" (verse 19). But he does not say, "Well done, good servant." He is not on the same level as the man who has gained ten. Like the parable in Matthew, one of them has gained nothing. He also is called wicked and his one mina is taken from him.

Earlier in Luke 19, when the nobleman hands out the minas, the citizens say, "We will not have this man to reign over us" (Luke 19:14). That nobleman does not forget that. So at the end of this parable, Jesus says: "Bring here those enemies of mine, who did not want me to reign over them, and slay them before me" (Luke 19:27).

Again, does that fit in with our picture of gentle Jesus, meek and mild? That gentleness is a true picture, but it is not the whole truth. Jesus is God's appointed judge. The one who gains nothing is called wicked, his mina is taken away from him and he is exiled forever.

The Sheep and Goat Nations

The fourth category of those feeling the impact of the Lord's return is found in Matthew 25: the sheep and the goat nations. Again, the passage is lengthy, but important.

"When the Son of Man comes in His glory, and all the holy angels with Him, then He will sit on the throne of His glory. All the nations will be gathered before Him, and He will separate them one from another, as a shepherd divides his sheep from the goats. And He will set the sheep on His right hand, but the goats on the left. Then the King will say to those on His right hand, 'Come, you blessed of My Father, inherit the kingdom prepared for you from the foundation of the world: for I was hungry and you gave Me food; I was thirsty and you gave Me drink; I was a stranger and you took Me in; I was naked and you clothed Me; I was sick and you visited Me; I was in prison and you came to Me.'

"Then the righteous will answer Him, saying, 'Lord, when did we see You hungry and feed You, or thirsty and give You drink? When did we see You a stranger and take You in, or naked and clothe You? Or when did we see You sick, or in prison, and come to You?' And the King will answer and say to them, 'Assuredly, I say to you, inasmuch as you did it to one of the least of these My brethren, you did it to Me.'

"Then He will also say to those on the left hand, 'Depart from Me, you cursed, into the everlasting fire prepared for the devil and his angels: for I was hungry and you gave Me no food; I was thirsty and you gave Me no drink; I was a stranger and you did not take Me in, naked and you did not clothe Me, sick and in prison and you did not visit Me.'

"Then they also will answer Him, saying, 'Lord, when did we see You hungry or thirsty or a stranger or naked or sick or in prison, and did not minister to You?' Then He will answer them, saying, 'Assuredly, I say to you, inasmuch as you did not do it to one of the least of these, you did not do it to Me.' And these will go away into everlasting punishment, but the righteous into eternal life."

Matthew 25:31–46

To understand this passage, we need to recognize that this is a follow-on from Joel 3, which gives us the setting. In this Scripture the Lord says: "For behold, in those days and at that time, when I bring back the captives [exiles] of Judah and Jerusalem" (Joel 3:1).

This is prophecy about the days in which we are living when the Lord is bringing back Jewish captives from all over the world. From more than one hundred nations, Jews have returned in the last fifty or sixty years to the land of Israel. Once, when I was in a language class in the Hebrew University, I discovered there were people in my class who had returned from thirty different nations. It is happening before our eyes.

Judging the Nations

The next verse in Joel describes another gathering that will take place in the land of Israel:

114

"I will also gather all nations [Hebrew, *goyim*, the word for *Gentiles*], and bring them down to the Valley of Jehoshaphat [which means "the Lord judges"]; and I will enter into judgment with them there on account of My people, My heritage Israel, whom they have scattered among the nations; they have also divided up My land."

Joel 3:2

Speaking here of the judgment of the nations at the close of this present age, God says, "I will judge them on the basis of how they have treated the Jews and the land of Israel." That is important to know. As we will see from Paul's teaching in a moment, this term *nations* or *Gentiles* is exclusive of the people of God. The Church faces a different judgment. In addition, we note that the Son of Man does not gather the Jews—only the Gentiles.

1. THE FIRST CHARGE

"They have scattered Israel." Historically, in fulfillment of prophecies by Moses in Deuteronomy 28, there have been two major dispersals of Israel into exile out of their own land. The first took place between about 720 and 600 B.C., when the Northern Kingdom (known as Israel) was taken into exile by Assyria, and then the Southern Kingdom (known as Judah) was taken into exile by Babylon.

The second dispersal, by far the greater, took place about A.D. 70, when virtually the whole Jewish nation resident in the land of Israel was either killed or driven into exile by the Romans. The majority of the Jewish people remained in dispersion until the State of Israel was reborn about the middle of the twentieth century. But even now only about one-quarter of world Jewry are again resident in their own land.

Anyone familiar with Jewish history during the past two thousand years would have to admit that Moses' prophecies of dispersal have been exactly and repeatedly fulfilled in nation after nation all around the world. Furthermore, we have to acknowledge that the fulfillment did not cease in biblical times or even many centuries ago, but that it has continued right into the present century. And the nations involved in that dispersal will be held accountable by God.

2. THE SECOND CHARGE

"They have divided up My land." We must remember, first and foremost, it is God's land. Secondly, it belongs to the Jewish people because God gave it to them by an everlasting covenant for an everlasting possession. Regardless of who is occupying it, the ownership does not change. It belongs to God and to the Jews. Let me hasten to add that God is not restoring the Jews because they deserve it. He is very clear about that: "I do not do this for your sake, O house of Israel, but for My holy name's sake" (Ezekiel 36:22).

In modern political language, dividing up is partitioning. In 1920 or thereabouts, the League of Nations assigned to Britain a mandate for the land of Israel, both sides of the Jordan. The terms of the mandate were to provide a national home for the Jewish people. In 1922, with a stroke of his pen, Winston Churchill signed away 76 percent of that land to an Arab nation then called Trans-Jordan, now called Jordan, and in that territory no Jew is permitted to live. So they divided up the land—76 percent to 24 percent.

In 1947 the United Nations, the successor to the League of Nations, arranged a scheme to divide up the land so that out of the remaining 24 percent Israel would get maybe 10 percent and 14 percent would go to the Arabs. What are they guilty of? Dividing up God's land. And those nations are going to have to answer for it.

I am British by birth, and I was living in the land of Israel when partition took place and when the State of Israel was born. I am an eyewitness to these events, and I will say that, short of open warfare, the British administration did everything in its power to prevent the birth of the State of Israel. But what happened? Israel was born and the British empire fell apart. Without ever losing a major war, the empire disintegrated. Why? Because it sinned against Israel and their land. This shows that God takes it seriously.

The Lion of Judah

Jesus begins this parable of the sheep and goat nations with these words: "When the Son of Man comes in His glory, and all the holy angels with Him, then He will sit on the throne of His glory" (Matthew 25:31). This is His throne of judgment, His throne as King on earth. Prior to this, He has been sharing His Father's throne, but at that point He will have His own throne on earth, the throne of His Kingdom.

> "All the nations will be gathered before Him; and He will separate them from one another, as the shepherd separates the sheep from the goats; and He will put the sheep on His right, and the goats on the left."
>
> Matthew 25:32–33, NASB

All nations will be divided into two groups: the sheep on the right and the goats on the left—the sheep to be accepted and blessed, the goats to be rejected and cursed. Here is the promise, first to the sheep: "Then the King will say to those on His right, 'Come, you who are blessed of My Father, inherit the kingdom prepared for you from the foundation of the world'" (verse 34, NASB).

Later we get His words to the goat nations: "Then He will also say to those on His left, 'Depart from Me, accursed ones, into the eternal fire which has been prepared for the devil and his angels'" (verse 41, NASB).

Two totally different destinies. One is blessed; the other is cursed. Notice the principle of judgment that separates the nations. First, the principle on which nations are accepted: "The King will answer and say [to these accepted nations], 'Truly I say to you, to the extent that you did it to one of these brothers of Mine, even the least of them, you did it to Me'" (verse 40, NASB).

Then the principle on which the nations are rejected: "Then He will answer them, saying, 'Truly I say to you, to the extent that you did not do it to one of the least of these [Jesus' brothers], you did not do it to Me'" (verse 45, NASB).

There is only one basis of judgment for the nations: their attitude toward and dealings with the brothers of Jesus. We know from Joel 3:2 that the use of *brothers* here refers to God's heritage—Israel. All nations are going to be judged by the way they treat and relate to the Jewish people.

Jesus did not become a Jew simply for 33 and a half years. He identifies Himself with the Jewish people eternally. In Revelation 5 we read how John has a vision of a scroll that has to be opened, but no one is able to open it. As John is weeping, one of the elders says to him, "Don't weep. The Lion of the tribe of Judah has prevailed to open it."

The title of Jesus in eternity is "the Lion of the tribe of Judah." *Judah* is the name from which we get the word *Jew*. In Hebrew *Judah* is *Yehuda* and *Jew* is *Yehudi*. There is only one syllable different. That is His title: the Lion of the tribe of Judah.

When we see rampant anti-Semitism throughout the earth, we had better give careful heed to our own attitudes, because all of us are going to be judged. From the picture in Matthew 25 of Jews without clothing, food or shelter, in prison and sick, it is clear there is going to be a tremendous worldwide upsurge of anti-Semitism. We already feel the undercurrents of it. God is going to permit it.

Yet notice this. What were the goat nations guilty of? Not showing mercy to the Jews. They did not actually persecute them; they just did not show mercy. Look again at their judgment: The King "will also say to those on the left hand, 'Depart from Me, you cursed, into the everlasting fire prepared for the devil and his angels'" (Matthew 25:41).

These are some of the most fearful words of condemnation Jesus ever speaks. The lake of fire was never prepared for human beings. We humans do not have to go there; the devil and his angels have no choice. We go only if we make the wrong choice.

Here is a principle about God's blessing and God's judgment. God blesses the Jews directly; He blesses the Gentiles through the Jews. As I have noted, all of us who are not Jewish owe every spiritual blessing we have to the Jews. But when it comes to judgment, God judges the Gentiles directly; He judges the Jews through the Gentiles. We can see this principle all the way through the Old Testament, and we need to assimilate it. God blesses the Jews directly; He blesses the Gentiles through the Jews. God judges the Gentiles directly; He judges the Jews through the Gentiles.

Completion of "the Spine"

We have viewed in this chapter four types of groups that will feel the impact of Christ's return—the first three within the Body of Christ and the fourth encompassing all the nations of the world. And with this passage we come to the end of Jesus' recorded words spoken to His disciples during those private moments on the Mount of Olives. This completes for us the Matthew 24–25 "spine" of biblical prophecy that Jesus provides—from the beginning of sorrows to the glorious picture of the King on His earthly throne judging the nations.

I want to turn now to various other Scriptures that connect with this framework. We will begin with Paul's teaching, which helps fill in the picture of the last days with frank and graphic imagery.

10

Fierce Times Will Come

One of Paul's prophecies begins in an unusual way for Scripture. "Know this," he says, "that in the last days perilous times will come" (2 Timothy 3:1). *Know this.* Usually the Bible simply says, "This is the way it will be." But Paul is so concerned that we should not have a wrong idea about the last days that he says, "Know this. Be in no doubt about this. Here is an absolutely established fact you cannot change by prayer, pleading or any other activity. It is going to happen, so bow before this fact." This gives us an idea of the importance of this revelation in Paul's eyes, and, as we will see, the picture he paints is not a pleasant one.

That word translated "perilous" occurs in only one other place in the New Testament: Matthew 8:28. There it describes two demonized men from the region called Gadara who confront Jesus after He crosses the Sea of Galilee, and it describes them as "exceedingly fierce." I would suggest that as a better translation also for the passage in 2 Timothy: "In the last days *fierce* times will come." We are living in fierce times. And they are going to get fiercer as things get worse.

Actually, it will not be so much "things" getting worse as people. People are going to get worse as they give in to the pressure to turn from God. One main source of pressure is the progressive degeneration of human character. Another is satanic spiritual pressure from the occult realm. Let's review these.

Degeneration of Character

Here is the initial description that Paul gives, following his injunction to "know this." As we read, let's again ask ourselves how many of these traits are conspicuous in our contemporary culture.

> Know this, that in the last days perilous times will come: for men will be lovers of themselves, lovers of money, boasters, proud, blasphemers, disobedient to parents, unthankful, unholy, unloving, unforgiving [irreconcilable], slanderers, without self-control, brutal, despisers of good, traitors, headstrong, haughty, lovers of pleasure rather than lovers of God, having a form of godliness but denying its power. And from such people turn away!
>
> 2 Timothy 3:1–5

When Paul speaks about fierce times, he begins with the root cause: "Men will be." Then he lists eighteen moral or ethical blemishes. In other words, human character is a root cause of the dark days to come—not nuclear fission or any-thing else. It is the moral and ethical corruption produced in humanity by sin. The appearance of these character traits will become more obvious and more blatant as this age draws to its close.

One word in this list from the New King James Version, the word *unloving*, is not really a good translation. The King James Version said it much better: "without natural affec-tion." In other words, even the normal love that we expect has evaporated in many cases. The love of a mother for her baby, the love of parents for their children, the love of broth-ers and sisters for one another. We do not have to look far to see that such love is evaporating rapidly. The basic cause is selfishness. It is an expression of self-fulfillment.

Notice that the list begins and ends with what people love: love of self, love of money and love of pleasure. These three loves are the cause of all the other negative attributes listed here, and they are interrelated. Why do people love money? Because they love pleasure. Money can buy pleasure, at least for a little while. But it cannot buy peace or joy. The love of money is also an expression of pride. Riches can encourage us to be arrogant, to display our wealth and act as if we are better than those who have less. These loves are rooted in love of self. That is the basis of what is breaking up our society today. What you love determines what you will be.

The love of self can be expressed like this: "If you don't like the way I live, I'll go my way and you can go yours!" That attitude dominates the thinking of much of the world today. It has broken up—and is presently breaking up—countless marriages. When marriage breaks up, the family breaks up. When the family breaks up, society breaks up.

The government can spend billions of dollars to find a remedy for society's ills, but there is only one: stable families. Children were designed to have two caring parents. If one of the parents drops out, it leaves unhappy, frustrated children who will possibly take out their frustrations on society. The generation that neglects its children is breeding its own source of judgment. The young people who have not been parented, loved and disciplined will grow up to plague our society with violence and hatred. It is frightening, but it is happening, and it is a tragedy. The root cause is self-love. All the other problems stem from it.

On the subject of marriage, let me note here that there is both a recipe for disaster and a recipe for success. The recipe for disaster is: "What will I get out of this?" If a person gets married on that basis, the marriage will be a disaster. The recipe for success is: "What can I give to this?" If a person goes into marriage with that attitude, the marriage will be a success. I had two marriages. The first lasted thirty years, until Lydia went home to be with the Lord. My second marriage, to Ruth, lasted twenty years, when she, too, was called home. Each marriage was a happy and successful partnership based on giving, so I am not basing this formula on theory.

"A Form of Godliness"

Paul next makes an amazing statement in this passage about the people who exhibit these blatant, evil sins. He says that they have "a form of godliness but [deny] its power" (2 Timothy 3:5). Even though he is describing people who embrace heinous sins, Paul states that these people have a form of godliness. The Greek word *godliness* is such that I doubt

Paul would have used it of any religion except Christianity. It does not lend itself to any religion that is un-Christian. Thus, he is saying that these people are professing Christians, but their lives have never been changed. They deny the power of godliness, the power of an encounter with Jesus to change human lives radically and permanently. A person can join a church, say a prayer, sign a form—and remain the same. But if that person ever meets Jesus, change will take place.

I met Jesus in an Army billet in 1941 during World War II. I did not have any doctrinal knowledge of salvation. I had no idea what the Gospel was. I was just an Anglican. There are some wonderful Anglicans, but I was not one of them. I never went to church voluntarily and I did not believe the Bible. But one night, about midnight, I met Jesus with such power that I ended up on my back on the floor for an hour, first sobbing and then laughing.

There was one other soldier sleeping in the same billet with me, a good friend, and I was laughing so loudly I woke him. I saw him get out from under his blanket and walk reluctantly toward me. He circled me a couple of times, keeping a safe distance. He finally said, "I don't know what to do with you. I suppose it's no good pouring water over you."

Something in me said, "Even water wouldn't put this out." That experience produced a radical change in my whole life, which has gone on for more than sixty years. Why? Because I met Jesus.

When people meet Jesus, they cannot stay the same. Someone can decide to become religious and join a church, yet remain totally unchanged. This is exactly what Paul says: It is possible to have a form of godliness but deny its power—the power to change people radically and permanently for the better.

Excluded from the Kingdom

We must now deal with a very sensitive but very important issue regarding these fierce days that are unfolding, so I want to include here passages from three different letters of Paul that address it. The first begins with the words *Do you not know?* I find that when Paul says *Do you not know?* most Christians today do *not* know. When he says, *Brethren, I would not have you ignorant*, most Christians *are* ignorant. This has gone on for nineteen centuries, and does not seem to have changed much.

Notice that Paul uses a key phrase in all three letters: *will not inherit the Kingdom of God*. It is one thing to be born again and enter the Kingdom of God, but it is quite another thing to inherit the Kingdom of God. A lot of those who have entered the Kingdom will never inherit it because they are living the lives that Paul describes.

Here is the first passage.

> Do you not know that the unrighteous will not inherit the kingdom of God? Do not be deceived. Neither fornicators, nor idolaters, nor adulterers, nor homosexuals [passive homosexuals], nor sodomites [aggressive homosexuals], nor thieves, nor covetous, nor drunkards, nor revilers, nor extortioners will inherit the kingdom of God. And such were some of you.
>
> 1 Corinthians 6:9–11

These people can be born again into the Kingdom of God, but ultimately they cannot inherit the Kingdom of God. They are excluded. We cannot inherit the Kingdom of God unless we repent. God does not admit any in this list without repentance.

God does not make exceptions for those who reject His commandments willfully. Paul says that these people will not inherit His Kingdom. But then he adds, and these are beautiful words: "But you were washed, but you were sanctified, but you were justified in the name of the Lord Jesus and by the Spirit of our God" (verse 11). Regarding our churches and fellowships, I am fully in favor of admitting prostitutes, homosexuals, murderers, drunkards—all—*if* they have been changed. But it is unscriptural to admit them if they are unchanged. And we have a right to demand evidence of the change in their lives.

Here is the second passage. Note that the majority of acts in this list are expressions of broken relationships.

> Now the works of the flesh are evident, which are: adultery, fornication, uncleanness, lewdness, idolatry, sorcery, hatred, contentions, jealousies, outbursts of wrath, selfish ambitions, dissensions, heresies, envy, murders, drunkenness, revelries, and the like; of which I tell you beforehand, just as I also told you in time past, that those who practice such things will not inherit the kingdom of God.
>
> Galatians 5:19–21

It is now fashionable to call fornication "premarital sex." But that does not change the nature of the act in the least. God still calls it fornication. One of the devil's subtle tricks is to put new labels on old things. So to kill a baby in its mother's womb is wrong, but to "abort a fetus" is supposedly different. In other words, some people believe that changing the word from *baby* to *fetus* changes the nature of the act. It does not.

In the third passage Paul again says that the people listed here have no inheritance in God's Kingdom.

> But fornication and all uncleanness or covetousness, let it not even be named among you, as is fitting for saints; neither filthiness, nor foolish talking, nor coarse jesting, which are not fitting, but rather giving of thanks. For this you know, that no fornicator, unclean person, nor covetous man, who is an idolater, has any inheritance in the kingdom of Christ and God.
>
> Ephesians 5:3–5

These three times in Scripture Paul says that such a person cannot inherit the Kingdom of God. He says to the Galatians, "I told you before, but I'm going to tell you again." I believe, brothers and sisters, it is time we tell people again. Standards today are changing, but God's standards have not changed. He is still the same. Changing the label does not change the act.

Upsurge of the Occult

Along with human degeneration into more blatant sin, another major root cause of times getting fiercer will be the operation of occult power. That is exactly where we are today. The occult has come out into the open. It is not hard to see that the powers of the occult are increasing—the boldness, the arrogance, the claims to superiority. Its use is aggressive and active to a degree that was unthinkable even twenty years ago. It is a fulfillment of prophecy.

Believers will be snared by the supernatural satanic pressure: "The [Holy] Spirit clearly says that in later times some will abandon the faith and follow deceiving spirits and things taught by demons" (1 Timothy 4:1, NIV). *Abandoning the faith* refers to Christians. Under intense, satanic, demonic pressure, some Christians will be deceived by demons and turn away from their faith.

In 2 Timothy 3 Paul explains further: "Now as Jannes and Jambres resisted Moses, so do these also resist the truth: men of corrupt minds, disapproved concerning the faith" (verse 8). The two names, Jannes and Jambres, refer to two magicians in Egypt who resisted and opposed Moses and Aaron. The conflict was not engaged in the natural. It was not a physical or even theological conflict. This battle was fought on the supernatural plane. In talking about Jannes and Jambres in relation to the last days, Paul is warning us today about the occult, the satanic supernatural—the "lying wonders" (2 Thessalonians 2:9).

This spiritual conflict is a similar situation to what happened when Moses and Aaron appeared before Pharaoh and said, "Let God's people go" (see Exodus 7:1–12).

Pharaoh replied, "What sign can you show that this message is from God?"

Moses told Aaron to throw down his rod, and before their eyes that rod became a snake. We might assume that would be proof enough, but it was not. Pharaoh said, "Wait a minute. I'll see what my magicians can do." Pharaoh called for them, and the Bible says they threw down their rods, which also became snakes. This sign was supernatural—but satanic.

Thank God, that is not the end of the story. What happened next? Aaron's snake ate the Egyptian snakes. Picture this: The magicians walked away with empty hands because they now had no rods. But Aaron's rod was thicker and stronger than it had ever been.

We must make no mistake: The battle for us in these last days is going to be just the same. It will not be a question merely of theology or doctrine: It will be a question of who has the power of God. This was predicted nearly two thousand years ago, and the prediction has not changed.

Notice Paul's use of the word *corrupt* in mentioning that people will become like Jannes and Jambres. There are two incontrovertible principles regarding corruption. All corruption is *progressive*—it does not get better; it always gets worse. And all corruption is *irreversible*—there is no way to turn back its working. I believe that these principles apply to the world situation quite well. The corruption in the world is progressive: It is never going to get better; it is always going to get worse. And it is irreversible; there is no way to turn back the process of corruption.

Paul says, "Evil men and impostors will grow worse and worse, deceiving and being deceived" (2 Timothy 3:13). The Greek word for "evil men and impostors" is *enchanters* or *wailers*. It speaks of people who cast spells by enchanting and wailing. Thus, we see the progress of corruption. Those ensnared by evil will grow worse and worse, deceiving and being deceived. No one is more successful at deceiving than one who is deceived himself. If he really believes his own deception, he speaks with conviction.

Now we could be discouraged at that fact. That would be one way to respond. But the other way to respond would be to thank God, because it proves the Bible is true! We can also thank God because the folly of those who are deceived will be made manifest to everyone, as was the folly of Jannes and Jambres.

Sometimes people want an excuse not to believe the Bible. They may say, "I don't want to become a Christian; there are too many hypocrites in the church."

When I hear that I reply, "That may be true, but the New Testament *tells us* that there will be hypocrites in the church. So their presence doesn't prove the Bible is false; it proves it is true. That is just one more reason for becoming a Christian."

We can say the same about these prophecies. We may think these messages are negative and dark, but they prove that the Bible is true. Also, if we can believe the dark it promises, we can believe the light it promises. But the point is that we cannot be selective. Every word of God is pure; no word of God is to be set aside.

God's Form of Government

It is undeniable that we Christians have an obligation to take action against the corruption of human nature initiated by sin taking its full course. But we also must believe the revealed prophetic word of God. Thus, with all due respect to most politicians and their usual promises for a brighter future, they do not have the solution. We cannot expect them to come up with a remedy for the problems of humanity—poverty, sickness, hatred, war—all of which are enormous and increasing. These terrible conditions are blighting the lives of millions of people. Still, we should pray for our government and our leaders within the parameters of the revealed will of God. (For more on this topic, refer to

Shaping History through Prayer and Fasting, Derek Prince Ministries–International, © 1973, 2002.)

I believe God is going to allow human wickedness to come to its full expression. If we are still alive, we will see real, innate evil manifested with ugliness and fearfulness hardly imaginable. God is going to let men and women, who claim to be able to choose their own leaders, make their own choices. The Bible reveals that ultimately one politician will rise to power with claims of solutions. That will be the Antichrist. But his answer will be worse than all the problems that have ever gone before.

Frankly, I prefer to live in democracy rather than tyranny, but we must realize this: Democracy is not God's pattern for government. *Democracy* is a Greek word, just like *humanism*, and it has corrupted our thinking. I was a student of Greek philosophy before I became a preacher, so I can provide some background. The Greek philosopher Plato gave a clear picture of different forms of government, an overview that is really hard to improve on. Starting with the best form of government and ending with the worst, here is his list:

The best is the rule of one good person, called *monarchy*. Another type is the rule of a few good people, called *aristocracy*.

Another type is the rule of the people by themselves, called *democracy*. (Abraham Lincoln, in his Gettysburg Address, resolved that "government of the people, by the people and for the people shall not perish from the earth." But he was wrong. It will perish.)

Another type of government is the rule of a few bad individuals, called *oligarchy*.

And the worst type of government is the rule of one evil individual, called *tyranny*.

Democracy is one of the weakest forms of good government. It is preferable to oligarchy or tyranny, but it is not God's model. God's form of government is monarchy—the rule of one good Man, whose name is Jesus. That is why I believe that a democracy is not the ultimate solution. It does not have the power to solve the problems of the human race. Men and women, basically, are not capable of choosing the right leader.

In the end there will be a monarchy. One Man, Jesus, will be King. He will lead a righteous rule, sharing His authority with His saints—those whom He has trained through suffering, affliction and discipline to rule with Him. Those people are called "the Church." Bear in mind that the word *church* is a poor translation of the Greek word *ekklesia*, which is essentially a governmental assembly. If we are members of the Church, we are members of a governmental assembly that will be headed up by one righteous Man, Jesus. There is no other valid solution for the growing darkness of the world than Christ's establishment of the Kingdom of God on earth.

A New People

We know, then, that corruption is progressive and irreversible. We know, also, that the attempt to redeem society without changing people is doomed to defeat. What is God's plan for His people?

God will not patch up the "old man"; He will produce a new creation. "Therefore, if anyone is in Christ, he is a new creation; old things have passed away; behold, all things have become new. Now all things are of God" (2 Corinthians 5:17–18). We cannot be in Christ and remain the same. Something totally new has happened that only God creates. Man can reform, man can improve, but only God can create. This is something God has to do for us and in us; we cannot do it ourselves.

I have heard people talk about redeeming the performing arts, but anyone who thinks that the performing arts can be redeemed without people being changed is deceived. God is not redeeming the old corrupt nature. It is destined for His final judgment. God's remedy is much more radical—it is a new creation.

Those of us who have experienced the new creation understand what it means. It took me months to discover what God had done in me that night in the Army billet. I really could not believe it, but it happened. I was a new creation. Please understand: I was not perfect, but I was different. That is what matters. A radical change had taken place. "If anyone is in Christ, he is a new creation."

God has a logical remedy for the old, corrupt, fallen nature. He does not patch it up; He does not improve it. He will not send the "old man" to church or Sunday school or teach him the Golden Rule. Simply put, God's solution is execution. The mercy in this is the fact that the execution took place when Jesus died on the cross. Our "old man" was crucified in Him. If we know that, believe it and act on it, it works. That is God's perfect remedy. It is a loving remedy, a merciful remedy. But it does not compromise with sin or with Satan. God will never do that.

Out of the new creation God is going to produce a new people. This is a proclamation I often make, and a glorious one at that:

> The grace of God that brings salvation has appeared to all men, teaching us that, denying ungodliness and worldly lusts, we should live soberly, righteously, and godly in the present age, looking for the blessed hope and glorious appearing of our great God and Savior Jesus Christ, who gave Himself for us, that He might redeem us from every lawless deed and purify for Himself His own special people, zealous for good works.
>
> Titus 2:11–14

As we have noted, God is going to take His own special people out of history. That is why He tolerates all the wickedness and tragedy and suffering. He is waiting until everyone He has chosen for Himself has come to Christ.

I was brought up a Brit. My family were all empire builders in India. Although they were good people, they were white and the people of India were not white. That made a difference. I remember as a boy of about twelve sitting at the table saying, "I don't understand why we couldn't invite an Indian to lunch." There was a deathly silence. I had said the wrong thing. Because I was the apple of everybody's eye, the only son, they did not squash me. But I realized at age twelve that they did not think the way I did. It is the way I have thought ever since. I am motivated to go where other people have not gone. Our ministry goes to some remarkable places. I tell you frankly, I like to see a congregation with a mix of people—different colors, languages and customs. That is where I am happiest.

All of us may not have the same feelings I have, but we need to let God enlarge our hearts. We can begin to pray for some nation. After we have been praying for a while, we will get a burden to see something happen with that nation. For the truth is, the age will not close until God has brought people from every nation, tribe and tongue into His Kingdom.

God has His chosen ones, and they come from every tribe, nation, people and tongue. Until they have all been reached, we cannot rest. That is God's remedy—a new creation that will produce a new kind of people who will be fit to share the throne with Jesus.

Remember, that is our high calling. And God is going to put us through everything necessary in these fierce last days, every kind of potential suffering or trouble or pressure, to make us fit to rule with our King. God has a solution, and that solution is the coming of Jesus.

11

Choosing Light or Darkness

We have been examining the picture the Bible paints of this world of ours as we draw near to the close of the present age. I now want to paint the backdrop to the stage on which the closing drama of the age will be acted out. In this backdrop there will be two contrasting color themes: on the one hand, dark and somber; on the other hand, brilliant and luminous.

The End Time Stage

For a general, overall impression of this backdrop of the close of the age, we turn to Isaiah 60. This chapter predicts the end time restoration of God's people in clear and beautiful language, but it also shows the background against which this restoration will take place. This is what Isaiah the prophet says to God's people:

> Arise, shine; for your light has come! And the glory of the LORD is risen upon you. For behold, the darkness shall cover the earth, and deep darkness the people; but the LORD will arise over you, and His glory will be seen upon you. The Gentiles [nations] shall come to your light, and kings to the brightness of your rising.
>
> "Lift up your eyes all around, and see: they all gather together, they come to you; your sons shall come from afar, and your daughters shall be nursed at your side. Then you shall see and become radiant, and your heart shall swell with joy; because the abundance of the sea shall be turned to you, the wealth of the Gentiles [nations] shall come to you."
>
> Isaiah 60:1–5

This beautiful passage has four main features. The first is that both darkness and light are intensifying at the same time. "Darkness shall cover the earth, and deep darkness the people." We see that happening—an ever greater spiritual darkness coming over the peoples of the earth. But in the midst of the darkness, "The LORD will arise over you [God's people], and His glory will be seen upon you." The message to God's people is: Respond to what God is doing. "Arise, shine; for your light has come! And the glory of the LORD is risen upon you."

The second feature is the regathering and restoration of God's people. "Lift up your eyes all around, and see: they all gather together, they come to you; your sons shall come from afar, and your daughters shall be nursed at your side." As we have noted, we are watching this being fulfilled literally

in Israel. And it is being fulfilled spiritually in the Church:
The glory of the Lord is returning, and the children of God
are regathering.

The third feature is that the Gentiles, or nations, turn to
God's people for answers. This always blesses me. I have
always been convinced that we who are God's people should
be part of the solution and not part of the problem. But so
often, it is the other way around: we are part of the problem
rather than part of the solution. Verse 3 says, "[Nations]
shall come to your light, and kings to the brightness of your
rising." I believe that is going to happen—nations and their
rulers are going to be at a loss for answers to their urgent
and pressing problems. Just as Pharaoh, the ruler of Egypt,
turned to God's servant Joseph for an answer, so in these closing days, nations and their rulers will turn to God's people.
And as we are illuminated by the glory of God and endowed
with the wisdom of God, we are going to have the answer
to their needs and problems.

The fourth feature is that the resources of the nations are
made available to God's people. "Then you shall see and
become radiant, and your heart shall swell with joy; because
the abundance of the sea shall be turned to you, the wealth of
the Gentiles [the nations] shall come to you." We need that
abundance and that wealth to carry out the tasks God has
committed to us. When the time comes—when we exercise
the faith, see who we are and what God's purposes are—a
tremendous abundance of resources is going to be released
to the people of God.

Returning to the scene of the backdrop, I want to point
out one other parallel feature of the close of this age. For this
we will look in the final chapter of the closing book of the

Bible. These verses show separation of the righteous from the unrighteous, bringing a situation where compromise and neutrality on the issues of righteousness will no longer be possible. These words are from Jesus Himself to John the revelator:

> Then he told me, "Do not seal up the words of the prophecy of this book, because the time is near. Let him who does wrong continue to do wrong; let him who is vile continue to be vile; let him who does right continue to do right; and let him who is holy continue to be holy."
>
> "Behold, I am coming soon! My reward is with me, and I will give to everyone according to what he has done."
>
> Revelation 22:10–12, NIV

The middle verse is sandwiched between two warnings about the closeness of the Lord's return. In verse 10, Jesus says, "The time is near"; in verse 12, He says, "I am coming soon!" But between these two is a challenge from the Lord to the righteous and to the wicked. It amazes me that the Lord would say, "Let him who is vile continue to be vile," but that is what He says. *The Living Bible* helps us understand it more clearly: "And when that time comes, all doing wrong will do it more and more; the vile will become more vile; good men will be better; those who are holy will continue on in greater holiness" (verse 11, TLB).

Here is the picture. The pressures are getting so strong that we are going to be caught up in one of two main streams: the stream of righteousness or the stream of wickedness. As these streams become more forceful, it will be almost impossible to escape from the stream we are in. If we are in the stream of righteousness, we will be carried on almost irresistibly by the power of that stream. But if we are in the stream of wickedness and rebellion, then we will be carried on in the power of that stream. Each will intensify. The righteous will become more righteous; the wicked will become more wicked. Two harvests are maturing at the same time: the harvest of righteousness and the harvest of wickedness. And Jesus tells us the harvest is the end of the age (see Matthew 13:37–39).

Both good and evil are intensifying. The gap between them is becoming wider and, ultimately, it will be unbridgeable. Every one of us needs to make a firm decision to be totally committed to God and to His righteousness.

Our Response

I want to suggest three appropriate ways to respond to the pressures and crises that confront us in the world—situations around us and coming against us. It is urgently necessary for God's people to know the appropriate response. What does God's Word reveal?

Optimism

I believe we are obligated to be optimists in the face of everything we see. In the gospel of Luke, Jesus sketches out a picture of events and trends that lead to the close of this age. He mentions much of what we have been looking at, and then, at the end of that discourse, He says: "Now when these things begin to happen, look up and lift up your heads, because your redemption draws near" (Luke 21:28).

Jesus does not say, "Be frightened" or "Look for a hiding place." He does not say to plan some method of escape and concentrate on survival. His attitude is, "Look up. Things are going to get better. Your redemption draws near." It is very important that we who are God's people present to the world the picture of confident assurance. That will impress them, and that will make them want to know what we have that they do not have—enabling us to face these pressures and crises with calmness and confidence.

We are obligated to be optimists. When we look on the situation in the world and compare it with biblical prophecy, we must remember that our attitude should be: "The glass is half-full." In other words, so much of what God has predicted in the Bible has already come to pass that it gives us a firm assurance the rest is also going to come to pass. The glass is on its way to being filled up, not emptied.

All these events and trends confirm the reliability of the Bible. If they did not happen, we would have to say the Bible is an unreliable book. But because they are happening— though there are many evils and forces against us—above all else, they confirm the Bible is a true, reliable, up-to-date book. It has a message that is relevant today, and that is vitally important.

Commitment

Our second response can be summed up in the word *commitment*. Total, unreserved commitment to God. One particular verse in Psalms expresses this, where the psalmist is speaking expectantly to the Lord about events that will bring the age to its close: "Your troops will be willing on your day of battle. Arrayed in holy majesty, from the womb of the dawn you will receive the dew of your youth" (Psalm 110:3, NIV).

The Bible is realistic: The close of the age is a day of battle, not a day of peace. And God has troops; God's people are His army, as revealed many places in Scripture, particularly Ephesians 6. When the psalmist says to the Lord, "Your troops will be willing on your day of battle," that translation does not carry the full force of the Hebrew, which actually says, "Your troops will be freewill offerings." We have an image here of God's people offering themselves to Him without reservation; putting themselves totally at His disposal with nothing held back.

We often hear it said that God wants our time, our talents and our money. That is not necessarily true. If we give those to God and think we are doing God a favor, we deceive ourselves. God is really saying, "What I want is you! And when I have you, I have everything you have." In these closing days, God is not going to settle for a lesser commitment. We need to ask ourselves: *Have I ever totally given myself to God without reservation? Have I placed myself at His disposal?* That is commitment. That is the appropriate reaction.

There is an alternative version for the second half of verse 3, one I believe is right. Instead of "Arrayed in holy majesty, from the womb of the dawn you will receive the dew of your youth," the alternative version, which I have studied carefully in Hebrew, is "Arrayed in holy majesty from the womb of the dawn your young men will come to you like the dew." I have a firm conviction that at the close of this age there will be a great army of young men totally committed to Jesus Christ, filled with the Holy Spirit, detached from the cares, ambitions, pride and covetousness of this world, set apart to God and arrayed in holy majesty. They will break forth out of the darkness of the past ages like something out of the womb of the dawn and they will come to Jesus like the dew. One of the most beautiful sights in nature is the dew on the grass in early dawn, as the slanting rays of the sun first catch those little drops of moisture and every one of them sparkles and is radiant. That is the picture of the young people that Jesus is calling to His side and to His service for this battle—the closing day of the age.

I want to challenge young people who are reading this—and remember, in God's army there is room for both men and women on the front line of battle. I encourage you to make that commitment to God, enroll in that army, because you are going to be on the winning side.

Those who are on the devil's side are backing a loser. If I were they, I would change sides just as quickly as I could and enlist in the army of the King of kings, the Lord Jesus Christ—the One who is going to win every battle He ever fights.

Alignment with God's Purposes

The third appropriate response to the situation in the world, closely related to optimism and commitment, is to align ourselves with God's purposes as He is working them out in the earth. If we do this, we are as unsinkable as the purposes of God. "The world is passing away, and the lust of it; but he who does the will of God abides forever" (1 John 2:17).

How true that is! The world is temporary; everything in it is passing away. It is impermanent, unstable, insecure. But the one who aligns himself with God's purposes, the one who is set to do the will of God, abides forever. Nothing can overthrow him or overcome him. God says, "I make known the end from the beginning, from ancient times, what is still to come. I say: My purpose will stand, and I will do all that I please" (Isaiah 46:10, NIV). When we align ourselves with God's purpose, we are aligning ourselves with something that is irresistible.

Two kinds of kingdoms are described in the book of Hebrews—the shakable and the unshakable:

> See to it that you do not refuse him who speaks. If they did not escape when they refused him who warned them on earth, how much less will we, if we turn away from him who warns us from heaven? At that time his voice shook the earth, but now he has promised, "Once more I will shake not only the earth but also the heavens." The words "once more" indicate the removing of what can be shaken—that is, created things—so that what cannot be shaken may remain.
>
> Therefore, since we are receiving a kingdom that cannot be shaken, let us be thankful, and so worship God acceptably with reverence and awe, for our "God is a consuming fire."
>
> Hebrews 12:25–29, NIV

The kingdoms of this world are shakable—they are being shaken and are going to go on being shaken more and more. There will be no stability, no ultimate security in any kingdom or system of this world. The unshakable Kingdom is the Kingdom of the Lord Jesus Christ. It cannot be shaken and because that is true, we are to "be thankful, and so worship God acceptably with reverence and awe, for our 'God is a consuming fire.'"

It would be foolish to give ourselves to a kingdom that is going to be ultimately overthrown when we have the option to give ourselves to a Kingdom that will triumph over all opposing forces. I would advise all reading this to accept my counsel and enlist in the unshakable Kingdom of the Lord Jesus Christ.

12

Israel and the Church

Two Covenant Peoples

Scripture tells us with clarity that God has two covenant peoples in the earth, two peoples to whom He is committed by a covenant He Himself has made. Those two peoples are Israel and the Church of Jesus Christ. Basically, Israel is formed out of natural descent from Abraham, Isaac and Jacob (whose name was changed to Israel). The Church is formed out of supernatural regeneration through the Holy Spirit, a creative miracle of God. Israel is a natural people; the Church is a spiritually regenerated people. Each is related to God by a covenant God Himself declares He will never break.

Here is a sample of what God says about His covenant with Israel: "Thus says the LORD, 'If the heavens above can be measured, and the foundations of the earth searched out below, then I will also cast off all the offspring of Israel for all that they have done,' declares the LORD" (Jeremiah 31:37, NASB).

God says that as long as heaven remains immeasurable and the foundations of the earth cannot be searched out, He will never cast off the nation of Israel or cause them to cease from being His covenant people. (Actually, it seems the more we try to measure the heavens, the more immeasurable they become.) God is saying that Israel is eternally His people. He will never cast them away.

Next, here is what Jesus says about the Church: "And I also say to you that you are Peter, and on this rock I will build My church, and the gates of Hades shall not prevail against it" (Matthew 16:18). *Gates of Hades* represents all the unseen spiritual forces of wickedness—Satan and all his kingdom. Jesus says, in effect, "I'm going to build My Church in such a way that no force of evil will ever be able to overthrow it or overcome it." It is an unchangeable guarantee of the continuation and victory of the Church of Jesus Christ.

Let's turn now to these covenants in greater detail, beginning with God's purpose concerning the restoration of Israel. We will follow with an exploration of His plan for the Church. When we understand these in the light of the Scriptures, we will have a much better grasp on the unshakable Kingdom of God.

God's Plan for Israel

Ezekiel 20, one Scripture out of many I could give, describes the unchangeable calling on Israel to be a people set apart: "What you have in your mind shall never be, when you say, 'We will be like the Gentiles, like the families in other countries, serving wood and stone'" (Ezekiel 20:32).

That is exactly what is being said at the moment. Recent governments in Israel have tried to obliterate the distinction between Jews and other nations. It will never work. God says it shall never be, and so it cannot be done. From the very time God created the nations and provided the earth for them to dwell in, His plan for all nations has centered around Israel, His chosen people.

> When the Most High gave the nations their inheritance, when he divided all mankind, he set up boundaries for the peoples according to the number of the sons of Israel. For the LORD's portion is his people, Jacob his allotted inheritance.
>
> Deuteronomy 32:8–9, NIV

There are certain elements of national pride and prejudice in most of us that would reject the fact that God made His plan for all nations center around Israel. But that is exactly what Scripture says. Israel was allotted her inheritance, and then all other nations were allotted their inheritance in relationship to it. We must remember that the inheritance, well-being and blessing of all nations come from and ultimately revolve around Israel. When Israel is out of her place, then all other nations are in some measure also out of order.

Let me give a simple example. Suppose as I start buttoning my shirt, by accident, I get the wrong button in the wrong hole at the top. What will happen? Every other button will wind up in the wrong hole. And when I get down to the bottom, I will realize something is wrong.

That is how it is with Israel. They are the first button to be placed in the first hole. If that button is wrong, then all other nations must inevitably be, in some way, out of order. They cannot be fully in their right place because it all starts with Israel. All other nations need to understand, therefore, that the restoration of Israel is really for their good. The well-being of all nations depends ultimately on the destiny of Israel.

Restoration after Devastation

In many passages of Scripture, God unfolds in precise detail how He is going to restore Israel. I will give a few quotations to show how exact these predictions are, and how they are being fulfilled before our eyes today.

> "This is what the LORD, the God of Israel, says [notice, He is the God of Israel]: I will surely gather them [Israel] from all the lands where I banish them in my furious anger and great wrath; I will bring them back to this place and let them live in safety. They will be my people, and I will be their God. I will give them singleness of heart and action, so that they will always fear me for their own good and the good of their children after them. I will make an everlasting covenant with them: I will never stop doing good to them, and I will inspire them to fear me, so that they will never turn away from me. I will rejoice in doing them good and will assuredly plant them in this land [the land of Israel] with all my heart and soul. [When God plants something with all His heart and soul, there is no power in the universe that can uproot it.]
>
> "This is what the LORD says: As I have brought all this great calamity on this people, so I will give them all the prosperity I have promised them."
>
> Jeremiah 32:36–42, NIV

Here is a clear, specific, down-to-earth parallel. Just as God brought upon Israel all the judgments—the dispersal, the agony, the exile and all else she has suffered for nearly two thousand years (and history gives us many details)—just as real will be God's restoration of prosperity to Israel. It is impossible to spiritualize either one. If the judgments happened in history and were fulfilled exactly, then the prosperity is going to happen in history and be fulfilled equally exactly. God says, "I'm going to change them. I'm going to inspire them with a heart that will delight to do My will and keep My laws. I will bless them. I will never stop doing them good."

We need to understand that the restoration of Israel is, initially, mainly political; ultimately, it will be very spiritual indeed. We see this in Jeremiah, where God says: "I will bring Judah and Israel back from captivity and will rebuild them as they were before. I will cleanse them from all the sin they have committed against me and will forgive all their sins of rebellion against me" (Jeremiah 33:7–8, NIV).

Notice the order. God says first He will bring them back to their land; second, He will rebuild them; and third, He will cleanse them and forgive them. The spiritual restoration is the climax. It is the ultimate objective, but it does not come first. At present, we are seeing the first part of that promise fulfilled. The second and third are sure to follow.

Another prophetic picture of Israel's restoration is given in Ezekiel 36.

"Therefore say to the house of Israel, 'This is what the Sovereign LORD says: It is not for your sake, O house of Israel, that I am going to do these things, but for the sake of my holy name, which you have profaned among the nations where you have gone.'"

Ezekiel 36:22, NIV

It is important to see that Israel does not deserve God's blessing and mercy. (Neither does the Church—let me emphasize that.) Both Israel and the Church are totally dependent on God's free, sovereign grace. It is not what we deserve, nor is it justice—it is grace we see in both cases. God says, "I am not doing it for your sake; I am doing it for My name's sake. You have profaned My name; I want to restore the honor of My name in you." He goes on to say:

> "I will show the holiness of my great name, which has been profaned among the nations, the name you have profaned among them. Then the nations will know that I am the LORD, declares the Sovereign LORD, when I show myself holy through you before their eyes.
>
> "For I will take you out of the nations; I will gather you from all the countries and bring you back into your own land. I will sprinkle clean water on you, and you will be clean; I will cleanse you from all your impurities and from all your idols. [Notice, they are regathered in spiritual uncleanness; the process of cleansing them and sanctifying them takes place *after* the initial regathering.] I will give you a new heart and put a new spirit in you; I will remove from you your heart of stone and give you a heart of flesh."

verses 23–26, NIV

I have many close and beautiful relationships with Jewish people. My observation is that God is taking away the heart of stone and giving back a heart of flesh capable of responding to His Word and to His Spirit. I venture to predict that we are going to see the dramatic spiritual renewal among God's people Israel within the near future. God then says:

> "And I will put my Spirit in you and move you to follow my decrees and be careful to keep my laws. [It is so important to see that neither Jew nor Gentile can do God's will apart from the Holy Spirit. Only when God puts the Holy Spirit in someone can he do the will of God.] You will live in the land I gave your forefathers; you will be my people, and I will be your God."
>
> verses 27–28, NIV

Every Christian who reads these words or hears them should rejoice. It is a testimony of God's covenant-keeping faithfulness to His people. It is a testimony of the absolute accuracy of the Bible. It is an up-to-date message that is being fulfilled before our eyes.

Getting the World's Attention

As God regathers Israel, it will serve as a sign that the prophecies given many centuries ago are coming true. Look at these words from Isaiah:

> In that day the Lord will reach out his hand a second time to reclaim the remnant that is left of his people from Assyria, from Lower Egypt, from Upper Egypt, from Cush, from Elam, from Babylonia, from Hamath and from the islands of the sea.
>
> Isaiah 11:11, NIV

153

What are those countries? Assyria is essentially Iraq; lower and upper Egypt we know; Cush is possibly Ethiopia; Elam is Persia or Iran; Babylonia is in the area between Iraq and Iran; Hamath is Syria; and the islands of the sea would be all the other continents and lands. These are all lands from which the Jewish people are returning. The prophet continues: "He [the Lord] will raise a banner for the nations and gather the exiles of Israel; he will assemble the scattered people of Judah from the four quarters of the earth" (verse 12, NIV).

Judah, as we have noted, is the word that gives rise to the name Jew. As God gathers Israel back to her own land, He also raises a banner for the nations—a declaration that the time has come. All prophecies that relate to the close of this age assume one thing: the presence of Israel as a sovereign nation in her own land. Until Israel was restored, none of those prophecies could be fulfilled. But now the stage is set. Here are just a few other prophecies along this line. If anything is clear in the Bible to me, it is this regathering process.

> "However, the days are coming," declares the LORD, "when men will no longer say, 'As surely as the LORD lives, who brought the Israelites up out of Egypt,' but they will say, 'As surely as the LORD lives, who brought the Israelites up out of the land of the north [Russia and Europe] and out of all the countries where he had banished them.' For I will restore them to the land I gave their forefathers."
>
> Jeremiah 16:14–15, NIV

> For thus says the LORD, "Sing aloud with gladness for Jacob, and shout among the chiefs of the nations [God wants this proclaimed among all nations]; proclaim, give praise, and say, 'O LORD, save Thy people, the remnant of Israel.' Behold, I

am bringing them from the north country, and I will gather them from the remote parts of the earth, among them the blind and the lame, the woman with child and she who is in labor with child, together; a great company, they shall return here."

Jeremiah 31:7–8, NASB

The Lord then orders His messengers to make a proclamation to all the nations regarding this regathering of Israel:

"Hear the word of the LORD, O nations, and declare it in the isles [the continents] afar off, and say, 'He who scattered Israel will gather him, and keep him as a shepherd does his flock.' For the LORD has redeemed Jacob, and ransomed him from the hand of one stronger than he."

Jeremiah 31:10–11

It is not to be kept secret and quiet. It is an occurrence God uses to attract the attention of the whole earth.

Is it not an amazing fact about Israel that this tiny nation of six million people is almost never out of the headlines of world news? Much larger nations carry on from year to year, and we hardly ever hear about them. But what happens in Israel is news today in all the media. The reason is that God is attracting the attention of the whole world to what He is doing for Israel.

God's message to the whole earth, to all nations, is that the same God who scattered Israel will also gather her. Just as the scattering is a fulfilled event of human history, so the regathering will also take place on the same stage of human history, before the eyes of all nations.

Warnings and a Promise

To further understand Israel's centrality, let us look back at God's original promise to Abraham when He called him to leave Ur of the Chaldees and go to another land—one he would later receive for an inheritance. This promise of God to Abraham is stated in the book of Genesis, a beautifully complete promise that has seven distinct sections:

"I will make you into a great nation and I will bless you; I will make your name great, and you will be a blessing. I will bless those who bless you, and whoever curses you I will curse; and all peoples on earth will be blessed through you."

Genesis 12:2–3, NIV

The fifth and sixth promises are particularly important and relevant to our present subject. "I will bless those who bless you," and "whoever curses you I will curse." We noted in chapter 9 that the destiny of all nations will be determined by their attitude toward Abraham and his descendants. The Jewish people are the touchstone by which all other nations are going to be judged, as we have stated in earlier sections. But it bears repeating.

Let us also remember that Jesus is a Jew, and the Jewish people, even in their rejection by God and their disobedience, are still the brothers of Jesus. So the dividing point between the sheep who are accepted and the goats who are rejected will be the way they have dealt with the Jews. Those who bless the Jews will be blessed, but those who curse the Jews will be cursed.

Scripture gives us a number of warnings in this regard. I want to relay two specific warnings to the nations about the way they relate to God's purposes for Israel—for the people, the land and the city of Jerusalem—and then relay a promise of blessing.

"May all who hate Zion, be put to shame and turned backward" (Psalm 129:5, NASB). Any nation that opposes God's purpose for the restoration of Zion will be put to shame and turned backward. That is the everlasting Word of God. It does not depend on the amount of oil they have or their armaments or any other factors politicians seem to take into account. God's eternal statement of divine purpose and judgment is this: "May all who hate Zion, be put to shame and turned backward."

In the Isaiah 60 promise of the restoration of Zion and of God's people, God gives this warning: "For the nation or kingdom that will not serve you will perish; it will be utterly ruined" (verse 12, NIV). Nations determine their destiny by how they respond to the restoration of God's people.

Now for the promise—a beautiful and familiar promise of blessing for those who align themselves with God's purposes for Jerusalem, for Israel and for God's people: "Pray for the peace of Jerusalem: they shall prosper that love thee" (Psalm 122:6, KJV).

We cannot merely take a neutral attitude and say, "Let's see what will happen." We have to actively identify ourselves with what God is saying in His Word and what He is doing in history. The primary way we can do so is to identify with what God is doing through our prayers. We can pray for the peace of Jerusalem. For the restoration of Jerusalem. For Jerusalem to become all that God has declared in the Scriptures Jerusalem shall be. To those who pray and are concerned, this is the promise: "They shall prosper that love thee."

PROPHETIC GUIDE TO THE END TIMES

The Hebrew word translated "prosper" does not pertain primarily to financial prosperity. It means they shall be at ease, they shall have rest, they shall have peace. There is an inner rest and peace that comes to those who, in the midst of all the turmoil of this world, associate themselves actively with God's purposes of restoration for His people.

God's Plan for the Church

In recent decades, there has been a dramatic increase in the activity of the Holy Spirit in and through the Church. This, too, is predicted in Scripture. Let us first look at the words the apostle Peter gives on the Day of Pentecost, when the Holy Spirit first falls on the waiting disciples in Jerusalem. As a result of the dramatic supernatural manifestations, a crowd of unbelievers gathers, exhibiting a variety of reactions. Some of them mock, saying that the apostles and the other believers are drunk, to which Peter gives this answer:

> "These men are not drunk, as you suppose. It's only nine in the morning! No, this is what was spoken by the prophet Joel: 'In the last days, God says, I will pour out my Spirit on all people. Your sons and daughters will prophesy, your young men will see visions, your old men will dream dreams. Even on my servants, both men and women, I will pour out my Spirit in those days, and they will prophesy.'"
>
> Acts 2:15–18, NIV

Note the phrase, *In the last days*. God says, "As this age comes to its close, I will pour out My Spirit on all people." The word used there literally means "all flesh"—the whole

158

human race. There will be dramatic, supernatural manifestations in the people of God. "Your sons and daughters will prophesy, your young men will see visions, your old men will dream dreams. Even on my servants, both men and women, I will pour out my Spirit in those days, and they will prophesy."

To understand those words more exactly, we need to turn back to the original source—the prophet Joel—who was quoted by the apostle Peter. The following two verses from Joel 2, when put together, provide a much fuller insight into the scope of this prophecy.

> So rejoice, O sons of Zion [that's God's people], and be glad in the LORD your God; for He has given you the early rain for your vindication. And He has poured down for you the rain, the early and latter rain as before. . . . "It will come about after this [God says] that I will pour out My Spirit on all mankind [all flesh]; and your sons and daughters will prophesy, your old men will dream dreams, your young men will see visions."
>
> Joel 2:23, 28, NASB

God says, "I will pour out My Spirit." Just previous to that, He gives the promise that He will pour out the rain that is due to the land. In other words, the outpouring of rain in the natural order is a type that illustrates the outpouring of the Holy Spirit in the spiritual order. Having seen this, we need to look more closely at what God says about the outpouring of the rain in verse 23. He promises to pour down the rain in two major installments: the early rain and the latter rain.

159

Rain—Natural and Spiritual

This is vivid to me as one who has spent a number of years in the land of Israel. If we understand the climate of that land, this prophecy assumes much greater significance.

In Israel, there are basically only two seasons: summer and winter. There is hardly anything one would call fall and very little one would call spring. During the summer season, the weather is completely dry. The summer normally lasts from about April until about November. This is approximate; there could be a difference of a month either way. Amazing though it may seem, during those months no rain falls at all. I spent one summer in Israel when there was absolutely no rain—until suddenly one night in October I was awakened by an unfamiliar noise. I looked out the window and realized it was rain. I had not heard rain for so long I hardly remembered what it sounded like.

At the end of the dry season, in the winter, there comes what the Bible calls the "early rain." The beginning of winter is marked by a major downpour that will extend over the whole country. After that, for the rest of the winter months, rain will fall. But normally it falls rather unpredictably—here a little and there a little, not covering the whole nation at one time—until the end of the winter. The end of winter is marked by what is called the "latter rain." It is the greatest outpouring of all, and again, it is normally universal—covering the whole land.

We see then that rain does not fall in Israel at all in the summer months. The early rain falls at the beginning of the winter, with unpredictable scattered rainfalls throughout the winter. The final, major outpouring of latter rain happens at the end of the winter.

All this is a picture of what God does for the Church through the Holy Spirit. We have seen that the outpouring of rain is, in a way, a prefiguring of the way God will visit the Church with the outpouring of the Holy Spirit. Particularly, it is emphasized in the writings of the prophet Joel.

The facts of nineteen centuries of Church history bear this out. The early rain, the first outpouring, which fell on the early Church in Jerusalem at Pentecost, probably lasted something like a century. For the Church at that time, it was universal. It affected every area where the Church was located. This supernatural visitation of the Holy Spirit was a normal part of Christian experience.

After that, using the terms of the analogy, there came the winter months of Church history. The Holy Spirit was never fully withdrawn—He was always active at some place and in some group, but there was no major outpouring of the Holy Spirit that affected the whole Church.

We move on then to the end of the winter season when the latter rain comes—that last great, final, universal outpouring of the Holy Spirit. I believe firmly that around about the turn of the last century, around 1900, the latter rain of the Holy Spirit began to fall on the Church and is falling today. I have had the privilege of traveling to all the continents of the world but one. Among many different nations, among Christians of almost endless different denominational and doctrinal backgrounds, my experience has been that this latter rain is falling on the whole Church. It is a visitation, a restoration of supernatural power and the fulfillment of biblical prophecy. We need to understand that we are living in the time of the latter rain. That realization will help us understand what to expect next.

The Outpouring of the Spirit

Let me illustrate this briefly from my experience training African teachers in Kenya for five years. My primary aim was to bring them the Gospel of Jesus Christ, the truth of the Bible. Early on, I found that they were really experiencing difficulty in accepting the Bible as a book for Africans. So I challenged them by saying, "I'm not going to try to convince you. There's only one way you'll know for sure if this book is really from God. If you experience the supernatural power of God in your own life, you will know that it didn't come from Britain and it didn't come from the United States. It came from God."

I continued to pray for them, and about six months later there was a supernatural visitation of the Holy Spirit upon that college of about 120 students, exactly as it is described in the book of Acts. One day I called the students together and I said, "Now your eyes have seen and your ears have heard everything that was written in the prophecies of the Bible about the outpouring of the latter rain. I'm serving notice on you: Now you know for sure this did not come from America or from Britain. It came from God." And I said, "This is God's testimony to you young people in East Africa that we are nearing the summer. This is the end of the winter. Next comes the summer, and the major feature of God's program for the summer is the harvest—the last great ingathering of souls into the Kingdom of God."

This is just one small example of how this specific sign— the outpouring of the Holy Spirit—is being fulfilled today in the Church of Jesus Christ.

God's Purpose: Restoration

In regard to both Israel and the Church, God is working toward one purpose. Though He is operating in different ways that are appropriate to the nature of the peoples, the purpose is the same: restoration. This is shown in Acts 3, where Peter says to the Jewish people:

> "Repent therefore and be converted, that your sins may be blotted out, so that times of refreshing may come from the presence of the Lord, and that He may send Jesus Christ, who was preached to you before, whom heaven must receive until the times of restoration of all things, which God has spoken by the mouth of all His holy prophets since the world began."
>
> Acts 3:19–21

Four successive phases, all related to the close of this age, are revealed in this passage. Interestingly enough, in the English language each of them is summed up in a word that begins with the letters *re*. The first is *repent*. God calls His people to repentance so they may come into line with His purposes. As long as we are stubborn, rebellious and unyielded, we cannot come into line with God's purposes. God says, "As you, My people, repent, there will come times of refreshing."

That is the second word, *refreshing*.

Next, God says these times of refreshing will lead us into the period of *restoration* of all things. So everything is going to be put back in its right place and right condition—particularly God's people. This period of restoration of all things is so important that God has spoken about it through each of His holy prophets from ancient times. It is the theme of all prophecy.

In connection with this period of restoration, the Scripture indicates we may look for the *return of Jesus Christ* from heaven. Those are the four words for us to anchor in our memory.

Repentance

Refreshing

Restoration

Return of Jesus Christ

The culmination of this period of restoration is a restoration of people, not things. These are the people of God, the peoples to whom God is related by His unbreakable covenants—Israel and the Church of Jesus Christ. This promise is the key to understanding the outworking of His plans. Although we see so much that is confusing, so much that might lead us to feel discouraged or downcast, if we can look below the surface, we see underneath it the strong, irresistible current of God's purpose flowing on to its fulfillment.

I love one particular Scripture that speaks of this restoration, and it has become very real to me in recent years. God speaks to His people and says: "I will restore to you the years that the swarming locust has eaten" (Joel 2:25). Oh, what a blessing! Can we truly grasp it? God says, "Not merely will I drive out all the insects that have eaten up your inheritance, but I will also give you back everything the insects have eaten!"

Let me illustrate this with an event from my ministry some time back. A woman was brought to me for prayer who was partially paralyzed in her left arm and leg. The left corner of her mouth was twisted up from paralysis, so among all else she endured, she was incapable of smiling.

I prayed with her, then I stepped back, and for ten minutes we watched God work a miracle. At the end of that period, she had recovered the use of her left arm and her left leg, her face was straight and she was able to give me a radiant smile. As we stood there just marveling at what God had done, the friend who had brought her for prayer said to her, "Why, you look ten years younger than you did ten minutes ago!" And I said to myself, *That's restoration! Ten years given back in ten minutes.*

Can we grasp the extent of the fullness of the promise of God from Joel? God is speaking to His people in these closing days: "I will restore to you all that the insects have eaten. Not just drive out the insects, not just get you back to Myself, but I will give you everything you ought to have—all the fullness of My blessing and provision."

It goes for Israel. It goes for the Church. It is God's promise of restoration to His people. In the midst of all the confusion and perplexity, it matters only that we know we are part of God's people. That His gracious purposes, His wisdom, His almightiness are all being exercised on our behalf to make us the people God wants us to be, that His name may be glorified and the nations of the earth may marvel at what God has done in us, His people.

13

Objectives of the End Time Church

In the book of Proverbs we are warned that where there is no vision "the people cast off restraint" (Proverbs 29:18, NIV) or "perish" (KJV). In a word, God's people need an ongoing vision to fulfill their calling. This is particularly true in connection with the Body of Christ. The Church is so high above man's natural concepts and plans that we absolutely must depend upon the vision given in Scripture by the Holy Spirit of what God has destined the Church to be. Only then can she do what she has been called to do: fulfill her objectives of unity and outreach.

God's Vision and Provision

One place where this vision is made gloriously plain is in the epistle to the Ephesians. The passage begins with an admonition to human husbands to love their wives, which is appropriate and necessary. But Paul uses the relationship between a man and his wife as a stepping-stone to a higher level of love—the love between Christ and His Church.

> Husbands, love your wives, just as Christ also loved the church and gave Himself for her, that He might sanctify and cleanse her with the washing of water by the word, that He might present her to Himself a glorious church, not having spot or wrinkle or any such thing, but that she should be holy and without blemish [blameless].
>
> Ephesians 5:25–27

We begin with Christ's double provision for His Church—the provision He made through His blood and the provision He makes through His Word. Simply stated: Christ redeemed the Church by His blood that He might thereafter make her holy by His Word. Each provision is absolutely essential for God's purpose to find its fulfillment.

Christ first gave Himself up for the Church by becoming the atoning sin offering. On the cross by His shed blood, He redeemed His people to make them a new creation, a new kind of people in the earth, a kind the earth had never seen or conceived of.

But His plan extended further. His final provision for the Church is thereafter to cleanse her, to sanctify her, to wash her with the pure water of the Word of God. This provision is just as essential to make the Church what Christ desires her to be as the shedding of the blood with which He redeemed her. If the Church is ever to become what God intends, she must be cleansed and sanctified continually by the precious water of the Word of God. There has to be a cleansing in every area of our lives: our thoughts, motives, imaginations, attitudes and relationships. All these have to be washed continually if we are ever to become the kind of Church Jesus has destined us to be.

On this basis, we see God's vision for the Church, what He has ordained it to be. The last verse of the passage on the previous page speaks about Jesus presenting the Church to Himself in all her glory—not having spot or wrinkle, but holy and blameless. The Church is to be permeated with the glory—the visible manifest presence—of God. Every kind of defiling or disfiguring characteristic, everything that would take away from her beauty and glory, has to be purged away, washed away, cleansed away. She has to become holy, set apart to God, mirroring God's holiness in an unclean and adulterous world. She has to be blameless, walking in the fulfillment of all her God-given duties, meeting every requirement of God. Only through the washing of the Word is this possible. Only as the Word permeates and penetrates our thoughts, our inner emotions and our inner being can we become that kind of Church.

Some people might say, "This is too much. It's extreme." Regardless, this is God's purpose. This is God's vision. God will never lower His standards to come down to man's standards. Even more, God has made provision to raise us up to the standard He has set for us.

Our Response

We see, then, God's vision for the Church: that she should be glorious, without spot or wrinkle, holy and blameless. We also acknowledge God's double provision for the Church: the redeeming blood and the cleansing water of the Word.

Clearly, this demands a response from us, both individually and as part of the Bride.

John helps us understand the individual response required from each believer:

> Dear friends, now we are children of God, and what we will be has not yet been made known. But we know that when he [Christ] appears, we shall be like him, for we shall see him as he is. Everyone who has this hope in him purifies himself, just as he [Jesus] is pure.
>
> 1 John 3:2–3, NIV

Once again, we start with a vision: We are going to be like Jesus. "Everyone who has this hope in him purifies himself, just as he [Jesus] is pure." This understanding keeps all our priorities in order, and we purify ourselves through the washing of water by the Word of God.

John also helps us with the response required from the Church as a whole. This is described beautifully in the book of Revelation, which portrays prophetically the climax of this age: the Marriage Supper of the Lamb. This is how it is revealed to John:

> And I heard, as it were, the voice of a great multitude, as the sound of many waters and as the sound of mighty thunderings, saying, "Alleluia! For the Lord God Omnipotent reigns! Let us be glad and rejoice and give Him glory, for the marriage of the Lamb has come, and His wife has made herself ready." And to her it was granted to be arrayed [to clothe herself] in fine linen, clean and bright, for the fine linen is the righteous acts of the saints.
>
> Revelation 19:6–8

This is a picture of the Church's corporate response: "His wife [the Church] has made herself ready." That indicates a process of preparation.

In my travels to many lands, and among many different cultures, I have attended many types of weddings. All over the world, I found one feature in common: It is the bride's responsibility to make herself ready for the marriage. And so it is in this heavenly marriage. The Bride's preparation is described in the final phrase: "The fine linen is the righteous acts of the saints." The beautiful garment the Bride must put on is a garment woven, not out of threads of linen, but out of righteous acts done in obedience to God and His Word. Each righteous act is one thread in the total garment that will clothe the Church and make her glorious.

The most important action for each one of us individually and the Church corporately is to find and fulfill the will of God, to see the vision God has for His completed Church and to bend all our efforts, prayer and labors—indeed, all we do—to the achievement of this glorious purpose of the Church. The reason? So that when Jesus comes, He will find the Bride as He determined she shall be.

The First Objective: Unity

There are two main objectives God has in view as He brings about the restoration of the Church. These divine objectives can be summed up in two words: *unity* and *outreach*. Let's look first at God's purpose to restore unity to the Church—or bring the Church into unity.

Jesus' Prayer for His Church

At the close of John 17 Jesus is brought to His arrest and to His trial. He is separated from His disciples and not restored to them until after His death, burial and resurrection. So, in a sense, what He says before these events are really the last words the disciples hear from their Lord before He is separated from them. I believe they are words of special significance. They form the High Priestly Prayer of Jesus to the Father.

In the first part of the prayer, Jesus is praying for the disciples who are then with Him. But in the closing part of the prayer, He launches out into a prayer for all future believers of all ages, all races, all denominations, all backgrounds. His glorious close to the prayer indicates His deepest longing and purpose for His Church: "My prayer is not for them alone [the disciples]. I pray also for those who will believe in me through their message, that all of them may be one, Father, just as you are in me and I am in you" (John 17:20–21, NIV).

I understand that to be talking about all true believers of all subsequent ages because, ultimately, if we analyze how believers come to faith, it is always through the message of the apostles. This message, recorded in the New Testament, is the only real basis for the faith of all believers.

What Jesus portrays here is one of many amazing comparisons in the New Testament. We previously saw the love of Christ for the Church compared to the love of a man for his wife. Now Jesus speaks about a bond of unity among all true believers, comparing it to the same relationship that exists between the Father and the Son:

171

"May they also be in us so that the world may believe that you have sent me. I have given them the glory that you gave me, that they may be one as we are one: I in them and you in me. May they be brought to complete unity to let the world know that you sent me and have loved them even as you have loved me."

John 17:21–23, NIV

Notice again, God's standards never fall to a position lower than that which is worthy of Himself. Jesus' standard of unity is the standard of the Godhead; the unity that exists between the Father and the Son is the unity Jesus prays for in the Church.

The Purpose: Love for the World

Let's notice two very significant phrases that appear there: "May they also be in us so that the world may believe that you have sent me" (verse 21, NIV); and "May they be brought to complete unity to let the world know that you sent me" (verse 23, NIV). Not only does Jesus focus on His own believing people but, as always, He has a deep compassion and concern for the world that does not yet know Him. He prays "that the world may believe" and that "the world [may] know" that God sent Him to be the Savior.

I believe in many different forms of evangelism and outreach. I am committed to them with my whole life and being. But I am realistic enough to know that all of them combined will never reach the whole world. Only one testimony can accomplish that: the visible unity of God's believing people. That ultimate testimony will cause the world to believe and make the world know that God sent Jesus.

Let's be realistic. This is not some mystical unity in another realm. It must be the kind of unity that this unbelieving world can apprehend with its senses. It must be a visible, demonstrated unity. That is the kind of unity for which Jesus prayed to the Father.

The Old Testament gives us a symbolic picture of this joining together into unity. It is a vision God gave to Ezekiel, usually known as the vision of the valley of dry bones:

> The hand of the LORD was upon me, and he brought me out by the Spirit of the LORD and set me in the middle of a valley; it was full of bones. He led me back and forth among them, and I saw a great many bones on the floor of the valley, bones that were very dry. [And this was a revelation of God's people; lifeless, scattered, separated.] He [God] asked me, "Son of man, can these bones live?"
>
> I said, "O Sovereign LORD, you alone know."
>
> Then he said to me, "Prophesy to these bones and say to them, 'Dry bones, hear the word of the LORD! This is what the Sovereign LORD says to these bones: I will make breath enter you, and you will come to life. I will attach tendons to you and make flesh come upon you and cover you with skin; I will put breath in you, and you will come to life. Then you will know that I am the LORD.'"
>
> So I prophesied as I was commanded. And as I was prophesying, there was a noise, a rattling sound, and the bones came together, bone to bone. I looked, and tendons and flesh appeared on them and skin covered them, but there was no breath in them.
>
> Then he said to me, "Prophesy to the breath; prophesy, son of man, and say to it, 'This is what the Sovereign LORD says: Come from the four winds, O breath, and breathe into these slain, that they may live.'" So I prophesied as he

commanded me, and breath entered them; they came to life and stood up on their feet—a vast army.

Ezekiel 37:1–10, NIV

What a beautiful picture of God's plan to draw His people into unity at the close of this age! Apparently, it began as a totally hopeless task. As Ezekiel walked up and down among the dry bones he must have said, "Surely, this is beyond help." Sometimes, we could feel the same about the condition of the Church: that she is beyond help—divided, scattered, weak, ineffective. Yet just as God gave Ezekiel the ministry that brought restoration and reunification to a scattered people, so His purpose stands for the Church today.

Two aspects of that ministry are significant for us. Ezekiel was told to speak certain words—to prophesy. The first time, he was told to prophesy to the bones. When the bones heard this prophetic utterance, they were changed—they moved and they came together. The second time, he was told to prophesy to the breath (or the Spirit of God). When he did, the Spirit of God came into those bones and they "stood up on their feet—a vast army."

I believe that "prophesying to the bones" represents preaching, but "prophesying to the breath" represents prayer and intercession. I suggest that both of these are desperately needed. The preaching of the Word will bring life and unity back to God's people. Prayer and intercession will bring the Holy Spirit back in His fullness into the Body of Christ and raise up scattered, separated, lifeless bones into a vast army.

In the Hebrew language, the phrase *a vast army* is emphatic: a very, very great army. Here again, we need to see

174

the objective. In this instance we are given a picture not of a bride but of an army—an army to do battle, to assail and cast down the strongholds of Satan, drive back his wicked forces and usher in the revelation of the glory of God to the whole earth.

My conviction is that the Lord Jesus never prayed a prayer that the Father will not answer. I believe God is going to answer that prayer of Jesus for the visible unity of the Church—a unity of the same type as the unity that exists within the Godhead between the Father and the Son.

The Importance of Leaders

The plan for this vast army is outlined in the epistle to the Ephesians, which speaks about the main ministries Christ has set in His Church, and the purpose for which those ministries are set there.

And He [the resurrected, ascended Christ] gave some as apostles, and some as prophets, and some as evangelists, and some as pastors and teachers, for the equipping of the saints for the work of service, to the building up of the body of Christ; until we all attain to the unity of the faith, and of the knowledge of the Son of God, to a mature man, to the measure of the stature which belongs to the fullness of Christ. As a result, we are no longer to be children, tossed here and there by waves, and carried about by every wind of doctrine, by the trickery of men, by craftiness in deceitful scheming; but speaking the truth in love, we are to grow up in all aspects into Him, who is the head, even Christ, from whom the whole body, being fitted and held together by that which every joint supplies, according to the proper working of each individual part, causes the growth of the body for the building up of itself in love.

Ephesians 4:11–16, NASB

Once again, we see the necessity of having a vision. The vision of the completed, mature, properly functioning Body is stated by Paul in verse 16: "the growth of the body for the building up of itself in love." This is the end to which everything God is doing in the Church is directed.

There are several practical and important points about this mission. First of all, when God wants to do something, He begins by finding people to do it. Jesus begins His program in the Church by placing leaders in these various ministries. Somebody said once, "God uses men, not methods," but that is not totally true. I would amend it this way: It takes God's men to apply God's methods. God works through leaders—they are an essential factor—and where there are no leaders to work through, the purposes of God are frustrated.

We see this in the record of how God delivered Israel out of her slavery in Egypt. We know from Scripture that Israel had been crying out to God in her sad plight for at least a hundred years. God told Moses He had heard their cry, but God did not move to deliver His people until He had a man whom He could trust—and that man was Moses. Then it took God eighty years to prepare Moses for that task. That shows us what tremendous importance God attaches to having a leader before He will commit Himself to a task.

As we look at the ministries mentioned here—apostles, prophets, evangelists, pastors and teachers—we notice that certain specific functions apply to them. The first is to equip the saints for their service. It is not God's purpose that those in full-time ministry shall do it all; that is a misunderstanding that has crept into some churches. It is God's purpose that those leaders shall equip the rest of the believers to do their own work. In one sense, the minister who does it all is really frustrating the purposes of God. It is much more important to equip others to do it.

The second is to build up the Body of Christ. These ministries must have the vision of the completed Body. All their labors and efforts must be directed to producing this Body, which is the ultimate vision and purpose of God.

The third purpose, which is the one most closely connected with our topic, is to bring us into the unity of the faith. Paul actually uses the words *until we all attain to the unity of the faith*. He is saying that this must become our objective, and it is dependent upon these ministries functioning correctly in the Church.

Paul also reveals how we will attain to the unity of the faith—through "the knowledge of the Son of God." Actually, the Greek word really means "acknowledging." It is not just an intellectual knowledge of Jesus as the Son of God, but it is acknowledging Him, giving Him His right place in every part of the Church and in every area of our own lives. That is the path to unity: that, as we acknowledge Jesus and give Him His rightful place and preeminence in every area of our lives and in the Church, which is His body, everything else will fall into line.

Doctrine alone is not enough. Every doctrine of the New Testament centers in the Person of Jesus. Salvation requires a Savior, sanctification requires a Sanctifier, healing requires a Healer and so on. It is not enough to have the doctrine; the doctrine must bring us into relationship with the Person. When the Person of Jesus is rightly acknowledged in His Church, then everything else will fall into its due place and order around Him.

The fourth purpose for these ministries is to bring us to maturity and completeness. A complete body: with every part present, every part doing its job. A mature body: not the body of a small child or a young person, but a mature, full-grown body.

As God sets these ministries in the Church—and it is His sovereign prerogative to do so—each of us must determine how we will respond. If we reject these ministries—if we are self-willed, stubborn, go our own way and do not submit to the spiritual authority God has set in the Church—Paul tells us what will happen: We will be like "children, tossed to and fro and carried about with every wind of doctrine, by the trickery of men, in the cunning craftiness of deceitful plotting" (Ephesians 4:14).

The implication is clear. If we do not come under these ministries, submit to their authority and obey their direction, we will continue to be spiritually retarded infants. We will be subject to every form of deception, carried hither and thither by every kind of new doctrine that comes along—never to attain real stability, maturity or responsibility.

On the other hand, if we submit to these ministries, the result will be love and right relationships and growth to fulfillment. Paul sketches out the pathway to this goal in verse 15: "Speaking the truth in love, [we] may grow up in all things into Him who is the head—Christ."

Our Attitude toward the Body

We must get in right relationship to the ministries, the authorities Jesus sets in His Church. That will put us into right relationship with our fellow believers. We will then speak the truth in love, and as we speak the truth in love, under discipline and authority, we cease to be spiritually retarded infants. We grow up into Christ. (He is always the ultimate objective.) We become members of that whole Body, which is fitted and held together by that which every joint supplies, where every individual part is doing its proper job. As a result, the Body grows naturally out of its own inner resources and life. It achieves the building up of itself in love.

God has a vision. God has a plan. God has a program. First of all, we have to hear the prayer of Jesus. Then we have to commit ourselves to the purpose of Jesus. Then we have to submit ourselves to the authority, to the ministry that Jesus sets in His Church. And then we have to come into right relationship with our fellow believers and become part of that total functioning Body. This will bring the Church into unity, which is one of God's divine objectives.

The Second Objective: Outreach

In the last chapter, we looked at a specific and distinctive sign of the end of the age that relates to the Church—namely, the outpouring of the latter rain of the Holy Spirit. Just as the rain in Israel comes in two main outpourings—the first rain at the beginning of winter and the last rain at the end of winter—so, historically, the Holy Spirit has been poured out upon the Church in two main visitations: the first rain upon the Church of the New Testament and the last rain upon the Church at the close of the age. It is my personal conviction that we are living in the time of the latter rain—that the present worldwide visitation of the Holy Spirit upon the Church is the fulfillment of that prophecy of Joel that God would send His people both the first and the latter rain.

In both cases—the natural rain and the spiritual rain—the purpose is the harvest. This is evident almost everywhere in the Bible where God speaks about giving His people rain.

In the case of the natural rain, then, we would expect a natural harvest—the ingathering of grain from the earth. In the case of the spiritual rain, we would expect a spiritual harvest—the ingathering of souls from fields all over the world. This is the great final ingathering of souls into the Kingdom of God through faith in Jesus Christ and through the ministry of the Holy Spirit. A passage in the New Testament makes this very clear: "Therefore be patient, brethren, until the coming of the Lord. The farmer waits for the precious produce of the soil [the harvest], being patient about it, until it gets the early and late rains" (James 5:7, NASB).

In the economy of God in the land of Israel, the harvest will fail unless the soil receives both rains, the early rain and the late rain. The farmer who is longing for that harvest for which he has labored so hard knows he has to be patient. As the rain does its work, the "precious produce of the soil" grows. He has to wait until the last rain has fallen before he can gather in that harvest. James drives home this application: "You too be patient; strengthen your hearts, for the coming of the Lord is near" (verse 8, NASB).

Rain for the Harvest

There are two important lessons here for us. Both the early and the latter rain are necessary for the harvest. As it is true in the natural, so it is also in the spiritual. The final great ingathering of souls into the Kingdom of God cannot take place until we have had the full outpouring of the latter rain of the Holy Spirit upon the Church all over the earth.

The second important truth is that the latter rain immediately precedes the Lord's return. In those two verses, James begins and ends with the theme of the Lord's return. He says, "Be patient . . . until the coming of the Lord . . . for the coming of the Lord is near."

Many Scriptures point to the same conclusion: the first rain on the early Church; the last rain on the Church of the close of the age; then the harvest, the great ingathering of souls into the Kingdom of God; and, in the time of the harvest, the return of the Lord.

Jesus says this Himself in a number of parables. We noted Matthew 13:39, for instance, where Jesus says, "The harvest is the end of the age." Another passage has the same message given with great urgency:

> "But this people [Israel] has a defiant and rebellious heart; they have revolted and departed. They do not say in their heart, 'Let us now fear the LORD our God, who gives rain, both the former and the latter, in its season. He reserves for us the appointed weeks of the harvest.'"
>
> Jeremiah 5:23–24

Why does God give the rain? Because without rain the harvest cannot be gathered. True in the natural; true in the spiritual. Why then is God pouring out the Holy Spirit upon the whole Church in fulfillment of prophecy? Because He has reserved to us the appointed weeks of the harvest. To me, this is a most urgent message. The harvest is never a lengthy period in any land; it is just a brief period. Any farmer knows that when the harvest is ripe you have just a few weeks either to gather it in or lose it. God has reserved those weeks for the Church in the earth today that the harvest may be gathered in. It is a matter of tremendous urgency. It is essential for our eyes to be opened so we can see the provision and the program of God and align ourselves with His purpose.

Explosions in the World

Let's expand our view of the harvest just a little further.

Our world is confronted today by a number of explosions—tremendous, sudden increases, upsurges. Here are four types.

First, a population explosion. The population of the earth is expanding at an alarming rate. I believe it is already past six billion and growing fast.

Second, the travel explosion. People have the ability to travel anywhere on earth in an amazingly short space of time.

Third, the communications explosion. The printing press brought in a spiritual revolution. What can we expect today from the sudden upsurge of communication innovations and media tools that have suddenly been placed at our disposal?

And fourth, the spiritual explosion. A worldwide outpouring of the Holy Spirit is bringing renewal, strength and victory back to the Church of Jesus Christ.

Let's paint a picture. Suppose in the midst of this population explosion, with all the facilities of travel and communication at our disposal, there was a tremendous spiritual explosion in the Church. Suppose the Holy Spirit was restored in His power and glory and fullness, the Church became united, equipped by the fivefold ministries, empowered by the Holy Spirit and then, in the purposes of God, was thrust out with this spiritual equipment and this vision into the ripened harvest fields in the world today. What would be the result?

It is very practical to estimate that in a period of five or ten years (or less), in those conditions, more souls would be gathered into the Kingdom of God than have been gathered into the Kingdom since Jesus died and rose from the dead. I believe that will be the harvest at the end of the age, the objective and fulfillment of God's purposes. We who belong to Jesus Christ at this time are obligated to see God's purposes and fulfill them. The book of Proverbs says, a son "who sleeps in harvest is a son who causes [his father] shame" (Proverbs 10:5). My prayer is that we will not be sons of God who sleep in the harvest and cause our Father shame. May we be awake to what God is saying and doing in our world today.

The Initiative Is with the Church

When we view the harvest from God's standpoint, we see that the initiative in world affairs is with the Church. Seldom do God's people seem to realize that. The initiative is not with the politicians or the scientists or the military commanders; the initiative is with God's people, the Church. God will never allow the initiative to pass into other hands while the Church is here as the representative of His Son, Jesus Christ.

We spent some time studying Matthew 24, the prophetic discourse Jesus gave while seated on the Mount of Olives overlooking the Temple area, in which He previewed the main events and trends that would mark the close of this age. We saw that the disciples asked the questions that prompted the answer Jesus was to give: "The disciples came to Him [Jesus] privately, saying, 'Tell us, when will these things be? And what will be the sign of Your coming, and of the end of the age?'" (Matthew 24:3).

As we recall, Jesus had just told them that the Temple would be destroyed, and the disciples, being religious Jews, could not conceive that the Temple would be destroyed without the age coming to a close. Of course, they were mistaken. The Temple was destroyed in A.D. 70, but the age has continued for two thousand years longer.

But let's focus once more on the latter part of their question: "What will be the sign of Your coming, and of the end of the age?" Again, we notice the question was singular: not "What will be the *signs*?" but "What will be the distinctive, sure *sign*?"

The Sure Sign of His Coming

In the next ten verses, Jesus gives many signs—but not *the* sign. He speaks about international wars, famines, earthquakes, pestilences, persecution of Christians, apostasy and betrayal among Christians, false prophets and cults, and abounding lawlessness leading to lovelessness. In this brief summary, we see He has given many signs, but not *the* sign.

184

But then Jesus addresses that specific question with a specific answer. "This gospel of the kingdom will be preached in all the world as a witness to all the nations, and then the end will come" (Matthew 24:14).

That is very clear. "What will be *the* sign of Your coming?" The answer: "This gospel of the kingdom will be preached in all the world as a witness to all the nations, and then the end will come." When will the end come? The end will not be provoked by the activity of evil, by the forces of Satan, even by human conflict. All this will play a part, but the decisive factor is the preaching of "this gospel of the kingdom . . . in all the world . . . to all the nations." When that has been done, the end will come.

Is there a specific day appointed for the return of Jesus? I believe there is. But I also believe certain things must happen first. I do not know the day. Nobody does. But we do know certain things must happen. How do we reconcile these two truths? Through the absolute foreknowledge of God. God knows when these events will have happened and He has appointed the day in the light of His foreknowledge.

We see a parallel in God's deliverance of Israel out of Egypt. He delivered one generation, but they failed to avail themselves of God's promises and commitments to them, so they perished in the wilderness. But the next generation entered the Promised Land. About four centuries before that, God had told Abraham when his descendants, the people of Israel, would enter the Promised Land. In His foreknowledge, God knew that one generation would fail, but He also knew that the next generation would succeed.

I believe the same is true of the Church. God knows which generation of the Church will succeed in fulfilling the task.

185

I trust and believe it will be our generation. This is the first generation in the history of humanity when all the technical provision is present by which we can reach the whole world in one generation. It has never been possible before. But with the explosions I have referred to—the explosion of population, travel, communications (and the power of the Holy Spirit)—it is technically possible now to reach the whole world in this generation with the Gospel of the Kingdom. I believe that is what Jesus intends and why He is bringing these facts to our notice so vividly by the Holy Spirit. That is why these promises and predictions are in the Word of God—that we might recognize the time in which we live and rise to our destiny.

God's Challenge to Us

Let us examine the Great Commission of Jesus Christ to His disciples after His resurrection:

> Jesus came and spoke to them [the disciples], saying, "All authority has been given to Me in heaven and on earth. Go therefore and make disciples of all the nations, baptizing them in the name of the Father and of the Son and of the Holy Spirit, teaching them to observe all things that I have commanded you; and lo, I am with you always, even to the end of the age."
>
> Matthew 28:18–20

There is a very important word here: *therefore*. We must never ignore the word *therefore* when we find it in Scripture. As I always say, "When you find a *therefore* in the Bible, you need to ask what it's there for." Jesus says, "All authority has been given to Me. Go *therefore*." Why "therefore"?

I understand it this way: The authority was given by God the Father to Jesus, the Son, after His death and resurrection. Jesus, in turn, here transmits that authority to His disciples. In other words, He is saying, "All authority was given to Me; now *you* go and exercise that authority on My behalf. The authority is vested in My name; as you go in My name, you have My authority."

Authority is effective only when exercised. A man may have authority and never use it, and no one would ever know that he had that authority. So it is with the authority we have been given by Jesus Christ. It is committed to us, but it is effective only when we exercise it. The only way the world will know the authority that has been committed to Jesus Christ as a result of His death and resurrection is when we, His disciples, exercise it on His behalf. Otherwise, the world is ignorant of what Jesus has actually accomplished; it does not know that the Father has committed all authority to the Son. Only through our obedience to Jesus' commission can the world ever be brought face to face with the fact that there is a king—a King of kings and a Lord of lords whose name is Jesus—and all authority is vested unto Him. We are responsible to demonstrate this to the world. As we go in obedience to the command of Jesus and bring His message, He will confirm it with the supernatural signs He promised and attest His own authority in the Word He has committed to us.

There is one other reason why He says, "All authority is given to Me. Go therefore." There are many places where it is very difficult to go. There are governments in the earth that resist or refuse the preaching of the Gospel. There are many closed doors today. But Jesus says, "If you will go and obey Me, remember I have the authority. If you will talk to Me about it, I will open those closed doors. I will make a way where there is no way. If you are determined to obey Me, I will make it possible to obey Me."

Safety and success for the Church lies in bold positive outreach. That means not getting frightened, not just looking for survival and not hiding in a cave with some hoarded groceries. The way to safety and success is bold, positive outreach in obedience to the Lord.

14

Arise in Victory

But thanks be to God, who gives us the victory through our Lord Jesus Christ. Therefore, my beloved brethren, we are steadfast, immovable, always abounding in the work of the Lord, knowing that our labor is not in vain in the Lord.

Based on 1 Corinthians 15:57–58

I have faced situations where it took all my strength to force those words out of my mouth. It took all my spiritual strength just to say those words because the pressures were so intense and the evidence of victory so absent. But it is still true, because it is the Word of God.

We do not want to squeeze through life, just barely surviving. We want to come through victorious. What will we have to go through on our way to victory?

Earlier, in Matthew 24 we read about "the beginning of sorrows" or birth pangs. Look at this list taken from verses

9–12, in which Jesus describes some of what we are going to go through in order to be victorious:

> They will deliver you up to tribulation and kill you.
> You will be hated by all nations for My name's sake.
> Many will be offended. They will betray one another.
> And will hate one another.
> Many false prophets will rise up and deceive many.
> Lawlessness will abound.
> The love of many will grow cold.

We learned from Paul's letter to Timothy that "in the last days fierce times will come." We are going to go through fierce times because

> men will be lovers of themselves, lovers of money, boasters, proud, blasphemers, disobedient to parents, unthankful, unholy, unloving, unforgiving, slanderers, without self-control, brutal, despisers of good, traitors, headstrong, haughty, lovers of pleasure rather than lovers of God, having a form of godliness but denying its power.
>
> 2 Timothy 3:2–5

Here is another typical Scripture on this topic: "As it is written: 'For Your sake we are killed all day long; we are accounted as sheep for the slaughter'" (Romans 8:36).

Who is killed all day long? Who is accounted as sheep for the slaughter? We believers are.

But that is only part of the story. Paul gives this promise: "Yet in all these things we are more than conquerors through Him who loved us" (Romans 8:37).

More than conquerors. I asked the Lord once what it was to be "more than conquerors." I felt the answer He gave me was as follows: "When you go into a trial you emerge from it with more than you took in. Not only do you emerge victorious, but you emerge with spoil." That is God's standard for us.

How Do We Get There?

How can we enter into this life of victory and fulfillment?

Do not love the world or the things in the world. If anyone loves the world, the love of the Father is not in him. For all that is in the world—the lust of the flesh, the lust of the eyes, and the pride of life—is not of the Father but is of the world.

1 John 2:15–16

The two loves spoken of here are mutually exclusive. We can have either the love of the Father or the love of the world, but we cannot have both. They are like oil and water: They do not mix.

John uses the phrase *the world* much more than any of the other gospel writers. Here is my definition of *the world*: all those who are not under the righteous government of God's appointed ruler, Jesus Christ. We may say, "There are some really good people out there, nice people." Certainly there are. But we ought to challenge them with one question: "Are you willing to make an unreserved commitment to the Lordship of Jesus Christ?" We will soon find out how nice they are! They may be nice in everything except that. "And the world is passing away, and the lust of it; but he who does the will of God abides forever" (verse 17).

All that the people of the world are scrambling for, craving, desiring and fighting for is passing away. It is impermanent. But the key for us to emerge victorious is this: "He who does the will of God abides forever." In other words, when we align ourselves with the will of God, we are as powerful and undefeatable as the will of God itself. That is the only key to victory and to emerging with spoil.

We have studied several purposes of God thus far. I want to conclude with three final instructions from Scripture, guidelines He is working out in the earth right now. These are the last pieces we need in order to understand our place in end time history.

Proclaiming God's Kingdom on Earth

The supreme statement of God's purpose in the earth at this time is found in the Lord's Prayer—just the first two verses, and especially the second: "Your kingdom come. Your will be done on earth as it is in heaven" (Matthew 6:10). Once I preached on the Lord's Prayer throughout central Europe—Hungary, Czechoslovakia and Germany. At each location, as I intended to tell them what the will of God was, I was struck by the opening words: "Our Father in heaven" (Matthew 6:9). I said to those dear people, "I hope you understand you have a Father. You are not abandoned, you are not left to yourselves, you are not of just a little worth. If you believe in Jesus, you are a member of the best family on earth. You never need to be downcast; you never need to feel inferior."

If we feel in some way rejected, unwanted, second-class, I just want to remind us that God has no second-class children. We are accepted by our Father in heaven. We are members of His family, and He really loves us. He knows our names, and He plans the best for us.

So guideline number one for God and His people is for God's Kingdom to come to earth and His will to be done here. That takes precedence over every other need and every other situation. Jesus came so He could bring God's Kingdom to earth. We are here as His servants and His people to assist in that process. It has to be the priority in our lives. It takes priority over earning money or eating or raising a family. It is the first item on God's list, and if we want to be in harmony with God, it has to be first on our list. "Seek first the kingdom of God and His righteousness," Jesus said, "and all these things [the things we need every day in life] shall be added to you" (Matthew 6:33).

In times of weakness, I have often failed God. But basically I can say I have sought first the Kingdom of God and His righteousness, and He has never failed to add to me the things I need. Pursuing things is not necessary—what we must do is commit ourselves to the Kingdom.

When we align with the purposes of God, God accepts responsibility for us. He says, "I'll provide for you; I'll open the doors." It is better to let God plan for us than to plan for ourselves. That should not mean we are indifferent or prayerless. By no means. But God's ways are higher than our ways. His thoughts are higher than our thoughts. The highest we can plan for ourselves is far below what He has planned for us.

The Gospel of the Kingdom

In Matthew 10 Jesus sends out the twelve apostles for the first time with this instruction: "And as you go, preach, saying, 'The kingdom of heaven is at hand'" (Matthew 10:7).

That is the message of the Gospel, and it is not often preached today. I have examined this many times, and, as far as I can tell, the apostles never held a healing service. They never held a service for people to tarry for the baptism in the Holy Spirit. They simply said, "The Kingdom of heaven is at hand. You can join if you like, if you meet the conditions." I do not mean to imply it is wrong to pray for healing; I have held many healing services. But I realize that was not the apostles' approach. Their approach was, "There is a Kingdom. If you meet the conditions, you can join. If you don't meet the conditions, you're excluded."

Then, as we have seen in Matthew 24:14, "This gospel of the kingdom will be preached in all the world." Not "this gospel of get your sins forgiven" or "you can be healed" or "speak in tongues," but "this gospel of the kingdom." The message has never changed. It started that way and it will close that way. It is a message of a Kingdom and a King.

Turning the World Upside Down

By way of illustration, let's look at the reaction of one group of people in the city of Thessalonica to whom the apostles came. As usual, when Paul turned up, there was a riot! It seems wherever Paul went, he had either a riot or a revival—or both. I was with a group of missionaries in East Africa once, and they were talking about opening a church in a new area. One of them said, "Let's make them mad or let's make them glad; but let them know we're here!" Those are my sentiments. The worst thing is to be ignored.

Soon after Paul and Silas arrived in Thessalonica, there was a riot. The people wanted to get hold of Paul but Paul's assistants had learned by that time to spirit him away, so he was not there. "When they did not find them [Paul and Silas], they dragged Jason and some brethren to the rulers of the city, crying out, 'These who have turned the world upside down have come here too'" (Acts 17:6).

Would they say that about us? That we have turned the world upside down? That we have upset things? Sometimes we are really too polite and too careful. We would do almost anything not to upset people, to maintain the status quo (regardless of the fact that the status quo is the devil's status quo).

> "These who have turned the world upside down have come here too. Jason [one of the new believers] has harbored them, and these are all acting contrary to the decrees of Caesar, saying there is another king—Jesus."
>
> verses 6–7

We learn a lot from the opposition. We see here what they thought about the message of Paul and Silas. The mob did not say anything about the forgiveness of sins or healing. They said, "These people are representing another king." Why? Because they were proclaiming the Kingdom. What upset the local authorities was that it was contrary to the rule of Caesar.

A brother from behind the Iron Curtain (while there still was an Iron Curtain) once said, "You can tell people, 'Jesus loves you,' and no one gets angry. But when you say, 'Jesus is King,' they'll put you in prison." Presently, most of us are not really declaring the essence of the true message: There is another King. This is the Gospel of the Kingdom: "There is a Kingdom coming and you can get into it or you can be left out of it, but you can't stop it from coming." That is a powerful message, but it does not always make us popular.

When the apostles proclaimed that message, all sorts of things happened. The sick got healed; demons were driven out. But they never had a meeting specifically for that purpose. They had one message: the Gospel, the Good News of the Kingdom.

We need to align ourselves with that. We are here to become part of the workforce that will bring in the Kingdom of Jesus Christ. I am completely pessimistic about human and humanistic solutions to world problems. Man does not have it in himself to solve his problems. The problems of war or sickness or poverty will not be solved by human plan. If I believed I depended upon humans, I would be a pessimist. But I am not, because I believe there is another Kingdom coming. It is not far away. There is a King coming who will reign in righteousness. Our highest calling is to align ourselves with the purpose of God—to proclaim and help to bring in His Kingdom.

Making Disciples All over the World

Our second guideline is closely related: We have to commit ourselves to the final order of Jesus to His Church, which is given in Matthew 28:19 and following.

I joined the British Army—not by choice, but by compulsion—on September 12, 1940. (I happened to remember the date because it was my mother's birthday.) The first thing the sergeant told us was, "Don't do as I do; do as I say." He had good reason to say that! But in the Kingdom of God, we cannot say that. We cannot give people instructions we do not follow ourselves.

Two other principles they taught me in the Army were: First, once an order is given, it is in force until canceled by someone in authority; second, ignorance of orders is no excuse for disobeying them. That is also true in the army of God. I smile when God's people talk about being an army. When I joined the British Army, under King George VI, I never got a certificate signed by the king guaranteeing that I would not have to lose my life. No soldier ever joined an army on that basis. And no solider has a right to join the army of Jesus on that basis. It may cost your life. Do not talk about being a soldier if your motive is self-preservation. Let's look again at these words of Jesus:

> "All authority has been given to Me in heaven and on earth. Go therefore and make disciples of all the nations, baptizing them in the name of the Father and of the Son and of the Holy Spirit, teaching them to observe all things that I have commanded you; and lo, I am with you always, even to the end of the age."
>
> Matthew 28:18–20

It is important to know who has all authority—not just some authority, but all authority. It is all vested in one Person and His name is Jesus. Having said that, and having cleared up the whole issue of authority once for all, Jesus commanded His followers to go and make disciples of all nations. Have we done that? By no means. Nineteen centuries have passed and we are still far from doing that.

I want to point out Jesus did not say, "Make church members." He said, "Make disciples." One of the biggest problems we have in the church is members who are not disciples. By their lives, they contradict the message we are to declare.

When we start a work for the Lord, we need to begin with disciples, not members. If we make disciples, sooner or later the members will come along. But they are not primary. The greatest single problem of the church in America is that we have made members who are not disciples. People might tell me that a certain church has so many thousand members. I say, "That's wonderful! How many of them are disciples?" A disciple is one who is under discipline. A disciple is one who has laid down his life. Jesus said that unless a man forsakes all that he has, he "cannot be My disciple" (see Luke 14:33). It is impossible unless we are willing to lay down our lives.

Baptizing Them

Then the passage says, "Baptizing them in the name of the Father and of the Son and of the Holy Spirit." We must understand that, properly practiced, water baptism is a commitment to discipleship. If people are not willing to be discipled, come under discipline and lay down their lives, they should not be baptized. Water baptism is as important in the New Testament as the baptism in the Holy Spirit. It is a decisive step. It is urgent. Jesus said, "Go into all the world and preach the gospel to every creature [not just all nations but every creature]. He who believes and is baptized will be saved" (Mark 16:15–16).

Neither should we fall for this line, "If you want to be baptized, we are having a baptismal service in two weeks; put your name down." That was not the attitude of the people in the New Testament. When God visited the house of the Philippian jailer (and His visit began in a powerful way—with an earthquake), I am sure He had the jailer's attention. When he and his family became believers, they were all baptized at that hour of the night. They did not even wait for dawn (see Acts 16:25–34).

When Philip met the eunuch on the road to Gaza (see Acts 8:26–38) and Philip got into the chariot, the Bible says he preached Jesus to him. It does not tell us Philip said anything about baptism. But when they passed a pool of water, it was the eunuch who said, "Look, here's water. What would prevent me from being baptized?" Philip did not say that he needed first to memorize Scripture and attend a Bible class, and, if he passed, at the end he would baptize him. No, Philip baptized him right away.

I was with a mission once that was a wonderful group of people, but they would not baptize anybody who had not been in a six-week baptismal class. The result was they were baptizing educated pagans! These people had been through the class, but they had never been saved; they just became religious.

So remember, water baptism is not a step we take somewhere down the road. It is part of our salvation. On the Day of Pentecost the unbelievers asked, "What shall we do?" Peter said, first, "Repent." Then, "Let every one of you be baptized . . . and you shall receive the gift of the Holy Spirit"

(Acts 2:37–38). And three thousand people were baptized in one day. That took a lot of hard work. If the apostles did all the baptizing, it must have taken several hours. But notice this: It made an indelible impression upon the people of Jerusalem. This is what it means to become a believer in Jesus. We have to go through the water.

Teaching Them

Then the Matthew 28 passage continues with: "Teaching them to observe all things that I have commanded you" (Matthew 28:20). The real teaching process does not come before baptism, but after it. When people have committed themselves to discipleship, we then begin to train them. But we must not train uncommitted people, because it is a waste of time.

I say all this from experience. I have seen the results both ways. In the church I attended in Fort Lauderdale, we basically operated by the principle that if you want to get saved you repent, you believe and you get baptized. They had a baptismal tank available every Sunday morning, and most of the people who were baptized in water also got baptized in the Holy Spirit.

There are people all around us who really would like to know how to meet with God. We must simply make up our minds that we are going to carry the Good News of the Kingdom wherever we go. We cannot be embarrassed or shy. If we offer a sweet smile on our faces, they will always be willing to listen.

In respect to taking the Gospel to all nations, let me just share an important passage from Revelation, part of a vision John the revelator had in heaven.

After these things I looked, and behold, a great multitude which no one could number, of all nations, tribes, peoples, and tongues, standing before the throne and before the Lamb, clothed with white robes, with palm branches in their hands, and crying out with a loud voice, saying, "Salvation belongs to our God who sits on the throne, and to the Lamb!"

Revelation 7:9–10

I pointed out already, but it deserves emphasis, these people were from every nation, tribe, people and tongue. The age will not close until there is at least one representative from every nation, tribe, people and tongue. God the Father will honor His Son, Jesus, for the sacrifice that He made. He will make sure there is one representative, at least, from every ethnic group, every language group, who has received the sacrifice and who is there to praise the Lamb.

Our job is not complete until we have reached every people group in the world. I am not directly connected in any way with the Wycliffe translators, but I certainly support them. They are taking God seriously because they have committed themselves to get the Scripture into every language spoken on earth, in line with this verse.

A People for God's Kingdom

We have looked at the first two main instructions of God in Scripture: He wants His kingdom to come to earth and He wants the Gospel to be preached to all nations. The third guideline follows logically after that: He wants a people for His Kingdom. Look once more at these verses:

201

For the grace of God that brings salvation has appeared to all men, teaching us that, denying ungodliness and worldly lusts, we should live soberly, righteously, and godly in the present age, looking for the blessed hope and glorious appearing of our great God and Savior Jesus Christ, who gave Himself for us, that He might redeem us from every lawless deed and purify for Himself His own special people, zealous for good works.

Titus 2:11–14

God is waiting for His own special people. Why does God tolerate the awful wickedness—the agony, the suffering, the poverty—all the terrible things that are going on in the earth? He could speak a word and stop it, but He will not stop it until He has a people for Himself. Jesus wants a Bride to share the throne. That is a main purpose of God—a people. They have to come from every nation, tribe, people and tongue. He wants a holy people, a purified people, whom He has purified from every lawless deed, from self-will, self-ambition and self-seeking, and zealous for good works. That is what God is after.

Concerning that, John tells us in his first epistle:

Behold what manner of love the Father has bestowed on us, that we should be called children of God! Therefore the world does not know us, because it did not know Him. Beloved, now we are children of God; and it has not yet been revealed what we shall be, but we know that when He is revealed, we shall be like Him, for we shall see Him as He is. And everyone who has this hope in Him purifies himself, just as He is pure.

1 John 3:1–3

The mark of those who really are waiting for the revelation of Jesus is that they are purifying themselves. How pure? Just as He is pure. God has only one standard of purity. It is Jesus. We may say we are looking forward to the coming of the Lord. But if we are not purifying ourselves, it is not true. It is the evidence in the life of every person who honestly and sincerely looks for the coming of the Lord.

How do we purify ourselves? Peter tells us: "Since you have purified your souls in obeying the truth through the Spirit in sincere love of the brethren" (1 Peter 1:22). We purify ourselves by obeying the truth of God's Word. It is not a mystical experience. What purifies us is obeying the Scriptures. What is the goal? Sincere love of the brethren.

Believe me, "the brethren" are not always easy to love! Bob Mumford used to say, "God has some strange children!" Then he would add, "And you may be one of them!" But that is the mark of purity: sincere love for the people of God. That is what will make us ready for the coming of the Lord.

Let me just recapitulate the three purposes of God with which we need to align ourselves:

1. The coming of His Kingdom on earth.
2. Proclaiming the Gospel to all nations, tribes, peoples and tongues.
3. Preparing a people for the Kingdom, God's own special people.

How Should We Respond?

As we said from the beginning of this book onward, though we see outwardly a tremendous decline in public morality, with abounding iniquity, lawlessness, violence and moral perversion of every kind—as the Bible clearly depicts—we also see the promise of victory in the midst of all of it. We find ourselves in a great spiritual battle with satanic forces in the background, with doctrines of demons, the working of evil spirits, the false prophets and, above all, the spirit of Antichrist in the background, causing what we read about in our newspapers—social, moral, political and international problems and decline.

Facing this, in light of all we have discussed in the previous chapters about the prophetic signs of the end of the age, we must ask ourselves these questions: What is God's plan and program for the Church of Jesus Christ? And what is our response to be?

Are we to sit by and fold our hands? Certainly, we could resign ourselves to say, "Well, all this was prophesied and foretold and now it is happening. There's nothing we can do about it anyhow. The whole world is in the grasp of the evil one. We'll just have to accept it. Maybe if we hold on we'll make good. Maybe we'll make the Rapture. Maybe we'll get through somehow."

Is that the attitude God would have us take? I believe not. I believe this is the hour for the Church of Jesus Christ to rise up in a new measure of victory, power and authority. It is our time to demonstrate that in the face of all Satan can do, God through His people is able to do more.

At various times in the Old Testament we see how Satan manifested his power. In Egypt he had representatives in the court of Pharaoh who could do miracles—they could change their rods into serpents and change the water of the river into blood. Let's not belittle this fact. Satan's representatives could do these things. But did God give up? No. He sent His own representative, Moses, to the court of Pharaoh, and Moses did all that the magicians could do and more. Whenever Satan moves in, God moves back with a countermove that is greater than all that Satan can do.

Likewise we remember the time in the history of Israel when the prophets of Baal dominated the land and they were offering sacrifice and worship. What did God do? He sent His man, His representative, Elijah. God said, "I'll show you that prayer in My name by My prophet will do more than all these prophets of Baal can ever do." God is never left without a response and an answer to what Satan may do.

The Standard Lifted

The latter part of Isaiah 59 says: "When the enemy comes in like a flood, the Spirit of the LORD will lift up a standard against him" (verse 19). God does not say the enemy will not come in like a flood. He says he will. But God says that when the enemy comes in, that is the time we may expect the Spirit of the Lord to have the answer, to lift up the standard.

In an ancient army, the standard bearer was the key person because he held aloft the standard of the army. All soldiers were trained in any time of crisis or confusion to look for the standard, to rally around the standard, to form themselves up and to launch a counterattack from the standard. As long as the standard bearer remained faithful and unharmed, keeping the standard up, it was a sure sign that victory was still possible. But if the standard bearer himself was ever wounded and fell and let the standard down, it brought confusion and panic to the army.

205

In Isaiah 10, describing a battle, Scripture says it shall be "as when a standardbearer fainteth" (Isaiah 10:18, KJV). When that happens, soldiers look around everywhere to see where they should rally, to see where the man is with directions and instructions for prosecuting the remainder of the battle. If the standard is gone, the army is confused and put to flight.

But it is different for us in this day of battle. For us, as the people of God in the Lord's army, the Holy Spirit Himself is our standard bearer. Just about the time when God's people might feel it is too much, things have gone too far, the earth is too dark, the forces of iniquity are too powerful—then the Bible promises, "The Holy Spirit—the Spirit of the living God—shall lift up a standard." When God's true people see that standard, no matter what church or denomination or background they may be from, they are going to rally around the standard bearer to launch a counterattack.

When it seems that things have gone too far, suddenly the Spirit of the Lord, in a way that has astonished us all, has lifted up the standard. God's people from every denomination and every background who really love Him and desire Him are rallying around that standard. We are seeing victory and not defeat for the people of God. No matter how dark the hour may be, even when the enemy comes in like a flood, the Spirit of the Lord is going to lift up the standard of victory.

We see this beginning to take place—the true ecumenical movement. Not a man-made organization, not meetings, committees and programs, but a move of the Spirit of God in His sovereignty lifting up a standard of the truth of God's Word and the Person and the work of Jesus Christ. Once again God's people are gathering around the divine standard bearer, the Holy Spirit.

Arise in Victory

Let's look once more at two verses addressed to the people of God by the prophet Isaiah:

> Arise, shine; for your light has come! And the glory of the LORD is risen upon you. For behold, the darkness shall cover the earth, and deep darkness the people; but the LORD will arise over you, and His glory will be seen upon you. The Gentiles shall come to your light, and kings to the brightness of your rising.
>
> Isaiah 60:1–3

God affirms in this passage that we are living in an hour when darkness is covering the earth, when deep darkness is covering people, and that darkness is going to increase. But in the midst of this time, the light of God's glory and power is going to come down upon His people in a new way. Great though the darkness may be, greater and brighter by contrast will be the light of God's presence and power upon His believing people. Though we must acknowledge the darkness of the time, let us not stop there. Let us declare that it is in the darkest hour that God will reveal His glory upon His people.

We have reached the stage spoken of in Revelation 22 where Jesus says: "He who is unjust, let him be unjust still; he who is filthy, let him be filthy still; he who is righteous, let him be righteous still; he who is holy, let him be holy still" (Revelation 22:11).

There is no more time or opportunity for compromise. The pathway of the righteous is going up toward the light. The pathway of the wicked is going down toward the darkness. We have truly come in human history to the parting of the ways. That is why many people do not like this present move of the Spirit of God. It confronts them with a need to make a definite personal decision. Am I going to set aside my prejudices, my preconceptions? Am I going to discard my carelessness, my carnality, my sinfulness, my lukewarmness? Am I going to follow through with God, or am I going to let the tide of iniquity and darkness engulf me and carry me right down into the gates of hell?

Each one of us has to make a personal choice in light of the situation that confronts us today. It is time to stop playing church and having a little religion on Sundays. This is not a game; this is a lifetime commitment. It is all or it is nothing, and there is nothing in between.

It is a privilege to live in these days, dark though they may be. For those of us who will believe God and catch the vision and listen to the voice of the Spirit, the end times are going to be a glorious time—a glorious time of victory!

APPENDIX

The *Thens* of Matthew 24–25

In interpreting this discourse of Jesus, one key word is used: *then*. It occurs numerous times in Matthew 24–25. This word indicates a succession of events following one after another systematically. That is the nature of this discourse of Jesus—it is systematic, thorough and basic.

Matthew 24

verse 9: "*Then* they will deliver you up to tribulation and kill you, and you will be hated by all nations for My name's sake."

verse 10: "And *then* many will be offended, will betray one another, and will hate one another."

verse 11: "*Then* many false prophets will rise up and deceive many."

verse 14: "And this gospel of the kingdom will be preached in all the world as a witness to all the nations, and *then* the end will come."

verse 16: ". . . *then* let those who are in Judea flee to the mountains."

verse 21: "For *then* there will be great tribulation, such as has not been since the beginning of the world until this time, no, nor ever shall be."

verse 23: "*Then* if anyone says to you, 'Look, here is the Christ!' or 'There!' do not believe it."

verse 30: "*Then* the sign of the Son of Man will appear in heaven."

verse 30: ". . . and *then* all the tribes of the earth will mourn, and they will see the Son of Man coming on the clouds of heaven with power and great glory."

verse 40: "*Then* two men will be in the field: one will be taken and the other left."

verse 45: "Who *then* is a faithful and wise servant, whom his master made ruler over his household, to give them food in due season?"

Matthew 25

verse 1: "*Then* the kingdom of heaven shall be likened to ten virgins who took their lamps and went out to meet the bridegroom."

verse 7: "*Then* all those virgins arose and trimmed their lamps."

verse 16: "*Then* he who had received the five talents went and traded with them, and made another five talents."

verse 24: "*Then* he who had received the one talent came and said, 'Lord, I knew you to be a hard man, reaping where you have not sown, and gathering where you have not scattered seed.'"

verse 31: "When the Son of Man comes in His glory, and all the holy angels with Him, *then* He will sit on the throne of His glory."

verse 34: "*Then* the King will say to those on His right hand, 'Come, you blessed of My Father, inherit the kingdom prepared for you from the foundation of the world.'"

verse 37: "*Then* the righteous will answer Him, saying, 'Lord, when did we see You hungry and feed You, or thirsty and give You drink?'"

verse 41: "*Then* He will also say to those on the left hand, 'Depart from Me, you cursed, into the everlasting fire prepared for the devil and his angels.'"

verse 44: "*Then* they also will answer Him, saying, 'Lord, when did we see You hungry or thirsty or a stranger or naked or sick or in prison, and did not minister to You?'"

verse 45: "*Then* He will answer them, saying, 'Assuredly, I say to you, inasmuch as you did not do it to one of the least of these, you did not do it to Me.'"

Subject Index

Scripture Index

219

25:24 211
25:30 103
25:31 117, 211
25:31–46 114
25:32–33 117
25:34 118, 211
25:37 211
25:40 118
25:41 118, 119, 211
25:44 211
25:45 118, 211
27:35 13
27:48 13
27:57–60 13
28:18–20 29, 186,
    197
28:19 196
28:20 200

Mark

13 46
13:32 34
13:33–37 35
13:35–37 81
14:50 13
16:15–16 199

Luke

2:4–7 13
9:26 77
13:26–28 104
14:33 198
16:15 107
17:26 85, 89
17:27–28 94
17:28–30 89
17:34 80
19 112
19:14 112
19:17 112
19:19 112
19:27 112
19:43–44 14
21 46, 47
21:9 52

21:20–24 48
21:23–24 49
21:25–27 49
21:28 141
21:29 82
22:37 13
24:46 14

John

1:11 13
4:22 64
5:1–9 13
6:15 80
10 79
10:12 79
10:28–29 79
13:18 13
14:23 110
15:16 70
15:25 13
16:13 96
16:13–14 41
17:17 75
17:20–21 171
17:21 172
17:21–23 172
17:23 172
19:36 13
19:37 13

Acts

1:8 19
1:11 34
2:15–18 158
2:37–38 200–
3:19–21 163
5:1–11 92
8:26–38 199
8:39 79
16:17 74
16:25–34 199
17:6 195
17:6–7 195
23:10 80

Romans

2:9–10 70
5:17 26
8:36 190
8:37 190
11:25–26 65
14 100

1 Corinthians

6:9–11 126
14:18 106
15:25 24
15:57–58 189

2 Corinthians

2:14 30
5 100
5:14 110
5:17–18 134
12 79
12:2 79
12:4 79

Galatians

5:19–21 127

Ephesians

1:4 70
1:19–20 23
1:20–21 23
1:22 24
2:4–7 25
2:5 25
2:6 25–26
4:11 99
4:11–16 176
4:14 178
4:15 178
4:16 176
5:3–5 128
5:18 105
5:25–27 167

221

Derek Prince (1915–2003) was born in India of British parents. He was educated as a scholar of Greek and Latin at Eton College and Cambridge University, where he held a fellowship in ancient and modern philosophy at King's College. He also studied several modern languages, including Hebrew and Aramaic, at Cambridge University and the Hebrew University in Jerusalem.

While serving with the British Army in World War II, Derek began to study the Bible and experienced a life-changing encounter with Jesus Christ. Out of that encounter he formed two conclusions: first, that Jesus Christ is alive; and second, that the Bible is a true, relevant, up-to-date book. These conclusions altered the whole course of his life, which he then devoted to studying and teaching the Bible.

Derek's main gift of explaining the Bible and its teaching in a clear, simple way has helped build a foundation of faith in millions of lives. His nondenominational, nonsectarian approach makes his teaching relevant and helpful to people from all racial and religious backgrounds.

He wrote more than fifty books, and his teaching is featured on five hundred audio and 140 video teaching messages, many of which have been translated and published in more than sixty languages. His daily radio broadcast, *Derek Prince Legacy Radio*, is translated into Arabic, Chinese (Amoy,

Cantonese, Mandarin, Shanghaiese, Swatow), Croatian, German, Malagasy, Mongolian, Russian, Samoan, Spanish and Tongan. That radio program continues to touch lives around the world.

For more information on Derek Prince and the many teaching resources available, please contact:

Derek Prince Ministries
P.O. Box 19501
Charlotte, NC 28219-9501
(704) 357-3556
www.derekprince.org